SAMS
Teach Yourself
HTML 4

Deidre Hayes

in **10 Minutes**
SECOND EDITION

SAMS

201 West 103rd St., Indianapolis, Indiana, 46290 USA

Sams Teach Yourself HTML 4 in 10 Minutes, Second Edition

Copyright © 1999 by Sams Publishing

All rights reserved. No part of this book shall be reproduced, stored in a retrieval system, or transmitted by any means, electronic, mechanical, photocopying, recording, or otherwise, without written permission from the publisher. No patent liability is assumed with respect to the use of the information contained herein. Although every precaution has been taken in the preparation of this book, the publisher and author assume no responsibility for errors or omissions. Neither is any liability assumed for damages resulting from the use of the information contained herein.

International Standard Book Number: 0-672-31721-4

Library of Congress Catalog Card Number: 99-63544

Printed in the United States of America

First Printing: September 1999

01 00 99   4 3 2 1

Trademarks

All terms mentioned in this book that are known to be trademarks or service marks have been appropriately capitalized. Sams cannot attest to the accuracy of this information. Use of a term in this book should not be regarded as affecting the validity of any trademark or service mark.

Warning and Disclaimer

Every effort has been made to make this book as complete and as accurate as possible, but no warranty or fitness is implied. The information provided is on an "as is" basis. The authors and the publisher shall have neither liability nor responsibility to any person or entity with respect to any loss or damages arising from the information contained in this book.

ACQUISITIONS EDITOR
Jeff Schultz

DEVELOPMENT EDITOR
Damon Jordan

MANAGING EDITOR
Charlotte Clapp

PROJECT EDITOR
Carol Bowers

COPY EDITOR
Jill Bond

INDEXER
Amy Bowling

PROOFREADER
Kim Cofer

TECHNICAL EDITOR
Coletta Witherspoon

TEAM COORDINATOR
Amy Patton

INTERIOR DESIGN
Gary Adair

COVER DESIGN
Aren Howell

LAYOUT TECHNICIANS
Stacey DeRome
Ayanna Lacey
Heather Hiatt Miller

Contents

About the Author

Deidre Hayes is an information architect with a Web services group that created and manages a very successful corporate intranet. She continually is looking for ways to increase productivity with online workflow techniques and has spoken to national audiences on her favorite Web-related topics: Information Design and Usability. She is a member of the Society for Technical Communications, the Usability Professionals Association, and the HTML Writers' Guild. This is her first book for Sams Publishing.

Acknowledgments

I would like to thank my family and friends who had to listen to me talk about this book for a long time. Thanks also to Randi Roger, Jeff Schulz, Mark Taber, and Damon Jordan at Sams Publishing for believing in me.

Tell Us What You Think!

As the reader of this book, *you* are our most important critic and commentator. We value your opinion and want to know what we're doing right, what we could do better, what areas you'd like to see us publish in, and any other words of wisdom you're willing to pass our way.

You can fax, email, or write me directly to let me know what you did or didn't like about this book—as well as what we can do to make our books stronger.

Please note that I cannot help you with technical problems related to the topic of this book, and that due to the high volume of mail I receive, I might not be able to reply to every message.

When you write, please be sure to include this book's title and author as well as your name and phone or fax number. I will carefully review your comments and share them with the author and editors who worked on the book.

Fax:	317-581-4770
Email:	`internet_sams@mcp.com`
Mail:	Mark Taber
	Associate Publisher
	Sams Publishing
	201 West 103rd Street
	Indianapolis, IN 46290 USA

Introduction

Since you're reading this book, you must have some idea of what HTML is, right? Maybe you already know that HTML is the language of the Internet and that far from being a complex programming language that requires years to perfect, HTML is actually a simple markup language that you can learn very quickly.

You're probably also thinking that if you knew how to create documents in HTML, you could help your company earn more money, or better yet, help *you* earn more money.

What you probably don't know is how to get started. How do you learn that language and what's it going to cost?

Getting Started

Guess what? You can create HTML documents on any computer system since HTML works the same on any type of computer. Even better, you can use software that you already own to do it. Any kind of text editor (like Windows Notepad) can be used.

Because we're covering a lot in 10 minutes, it will certainly help as you go through this book if you already have some basic computer skills, including the ability to use a word processor, some understanding of how to use directories and filenames on your computer system, and some experience using a Web browser like Netscape or Internet Explorer.

What Is the *Sams Teach Yourself in 10 Minutes* Series?

Sams Teach Yourself HTML 4.0 in 10 Minutes uses a series of lessons that walk you through the basics of HTML, then moves on to more advanced features of the language. Each lesson is designed to take about 10 minutes, and each is limited to a particular feature, or several related features, of the HTML language. There are plenty of examples and screen shots to show you what things look like. By the time you finish this book, you should feel confident in creating your own HTML documents for the World Wide Web. You can even use HTML to provide unique and valuable services to your organization, or to tell the world about yourself.

Special Sidebars

In addition to the explanatory text and other helpful tidbits in this book, you will find icons that highlight special kinds of information.

 Plain English sidebars appear whenever a new term is defined. If you aren't familiar with terms and concepts, watch for these flagged paragraphs.

 Caution sidebars alert you to common mistakes and tell you how to avoid them. These paragraphs also explain how to undo certain features, and highlight remaining differences in HTML.

 Tip sidebars explain shortcuts (for example, key combinations) for performing certain tasks.

Conventions Used in this Book

The creation and editing of HTML documents can be done using any of a wide variety of editing tools. As a result, this book doesn't use the "press-this-key" or "type-in-this-command" format common in the other books in the *Sams Teach Yourself in 10 Minutes* series. Rather, you'll find many excerpts from HTML documents that illustrate points being made. These fragments look like this:

```
<HTML>
<HEAD><TITLE>This is the Title of Your Page</TITLE></HEAD>
<BODY>This is the document text surrounded by HTML
tags.</BODY>
</HTML>
```

If you're working along with the examples, you may want to enter the HTML fragments into your own HTML documents as you work through the lessons.

Some easy-to-identify elements throughout the book:

What you type/ HTML fragments	HTML examples and excerpts you can type appear in **bold** type.
New/Important terms	Terms you should pay special attention to also appear in **bold** type.
Items you select	Commands, options, and icons you select as well as keys you press appear in blue.

Web Browsers Screen Shots

Web browsers (like Internet Explorer and Netscape) are used to interpret HTML documents for your computer. There are many different types of Web browsers (some with more bells and whistles, some with less), but they all do essentially the same thing. You'll find out about some of these differences (and how to avoid problems) as we move through the lessons in this book. To avoid confusion, all of the Web browser screen shots in this book were taken from Internet Explorer.

LESSON 1
Why Is HTML So Great?

In this lesson, you will learn how the Internet works and why HTML is so important.

What Is the Internet?

Like many inventions, the Internet began as the solution to a problem. It began with the government's need to find a way to link several computer networks together to share files—in other words, to create a network of networks. These computer networks were located all over the world and sharing information the old fashioned way took a long time. Today, the idea of sharing files with people around the world doesn't sound like such a big deal when almost everyone has a modem, email, and dial-up connections that make Wide Area Networks (WANs) commonplace. Back then, however, non one had even considered the idea. So, how did they do it? Well, researchers working for the Advanced Research Projects Agency (ARPA) created ARPAnet, which was essentially the first WAN. Eventually, this led to an *Internet Protocol* (IP)—a common computer language, or protocol—that enables all computers to talk to each other.

 Internet Protocol (IP)   A predefined process used to enable computers to communicate with each other, regardless of which operating system they are running.

This protocol and the new "network of networks" made exchanging information much easier than ever before, but it still wasn't simple. In order to find information on the Internet, you had to know where it was stored.

You first had to understand how all the computers were connected and then you had to navigate through the network to find the data you were looking for.

All that changed in the early 1990s. At that time, a new protocol was created. That protocol, the *Hypertext Transfer Protocol* (HTTP), enabled information on the Internet to be accessed individually; it's what allows you to jump from one Web page to another by pointing and clicking. The code that makes up the HTTP protocol was a breakthrough; however, it can't do everything by itself. The information stored on the computers in the network (the documents and data that can be found) must include its own set of communication tools so that the other computers in the network can interpret the information. In the case of the World Wide Web, the communication tool is *HTML*.

 HTML   Stands for HyperText Markup Language. All documents that appear on the World Wide Web were written in HTML.

What Is HTML?

In the introduction, you learned that HTML was a markup language, not a programming language. In fact, the word *HTML* is actually an acronym that stands for HyperText Markup Language. You can apply this markup language to text, images, sound and movie files, and almost any other type of electronic information. You use the language to format documents and link them together, regardless of the type of computer with which the file originally was created.

Why is that important? You know that if you write a document in your favorite word processor and you send it to a friend that doesn't have that same word processor, your friend can't read the document, right? The same is true for almost any type of file, including spreadsheets, databases, and bookkeeping software. Rather than using some proprietary programming code that can be interpreted by a specific software program only, HTML is written as plain text that any Web browser or word processing software can read. It does this by using predefined commands to determine how pieces of the document should look. These commands, called *tags*, are defined by the *World Wide Web Consortium*. You'll learn more about tags in upcoming chapters.

> **HTML tags**   These are commands that are used to define how pieces of an HTML document should look. They most often are used in pairs to surround the text they are defining.

> **World Wide Web Consortium (W3C)**   Members of this group develop the protocols that make up the World Wide Web. Currently, the W3C has 180 members from commercial, academic, and governmental organizations worldwide.

How Does It Work?

A markup language such as HTML serves another important purpose when it comes to sharing information over long distances: it separates the text from the format of that text. This means that information comes to you faster because your computer (using a Web browser) does the work of interpreting the format after you receive the page. Sound confusing? Well, let's look at it another way.

Your computer has a Web browser, such as Internet Explorer or Netscape Navigator, installed on it. When you are looking for information on the Web, your browser has to find the computer that is storing that information. It does this using the HTTP protocol. That storage computer, or *server*, then sends the new Web page (as a plain text file) back to your computer using the same HTTP protocol. Your browser sees the new Web page and interprets the text and HTML tags to show you the formatting, graphics, and text that appear on the page.

> **Tip**   HTTP isn't the only protocol used on the Internet. Each protocol is used for a specific network service, such as electronic mail or file transfers. The HTTP protocol was designed to combine many of these network protocols so that you don't have to learn all of them.

Getting Connected

It may be apparent, but sometimes it pays to state the obvious. Although you can create Web page files in any plain text editor and view them in any browser, you have to decide how you are going to store the files. You already know that you can't "surf the Net" without having an *Internet Service Provider* (ISP). In the same way, you'll need a *Web host* server that stores your pages before they can be viewed from the Web. However, other ways to view Web pages exist. Table 1.1 describes the methods you can use to store your files.

TABLE 1.1   Storing and Viewing Your Documents

If you store your files on	They can be viewed by people with access to
Your own computer	Your computer (or an *intranet*)
A disk or CD-ROM	That disk or CD-ROM
A Web host server	The World Wide Web

Internet Service Provider (ISP)   A company that provides you with access to the Internet.

Intranet   This is like your own private Internet in that it uses the same HTTP protocol as the World Wide Web, but it is accessible only by people within your own network.

 Web Host   A company that stores (hosts) information that can be accessed from the Internet using the HTTP protocol. A Web host may also be called a *Web Presence Provider* (WPP).

In this lesson, you've learned:

- HTML is a markup language that defines the structure, rather than the format of the text elements in your documents.

- HTML is platform-independent. As long as they have a browser, your Web site visitors can see the same Web page on a PC, Macintosh, or UNIX computer.

- You'll need a *Web host* server that stores your pages before they can be viewed from the Web.

LESSON 2
Creating Your First Page

In this lesson, you will learn to create, save, and view simple Web pages.

Getting Started

I think you'll find that the best way to learn is to follow along with the examples in this book and create your own Web pages as you read. As you learned in the introduction of this book, you can create Web pages, or HTML documents, with any text editor, including Microsoft Notepad, DOS edit, Mac SimpleText, and UNIX vi. You probably already have at least one of these editors installed on your computer, even if you have never used it before.

> **Caution** Although you also can create Web pages using some word processors (such as Microsoft Word) and some *WYSIWYG* programs (such as Microsoft FrontPage), I suggest you ignore those programs for now and concentrate on learning HTML, not a new program. HTML authoring tools will be discussed in Chapter 16, "Web Page Authoring Tools."

> **WYSIWYG**   An acronym for What You See Is What You Get. It generally refers to software programs that enable you to see what the page will look like without seeing all of the program's formatting codes.

Required Elements

To see what HTML looks like and learn the most basic HTML tags, let's look at a very simple HTML document. Figure 2.1 shows a simple Web page in Windows Notepad. You can type the same text in your own editor to follow along with the lesson.

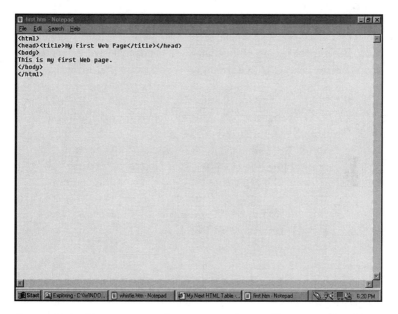

FIGURE 2.1   The <html> and </html> tags are all you need to identify your file as an HTML file.

Every HTML document must begin with the <html> tag and end with its pair, the </html> tag. In addition to the <html> tag, this document includes three other pairs of tags that should be included in any HTML document.

- The <head> and </head> tags are used to indicate any information about the document itself. You'll learn how to add some of this information in later chapters.

- The <title> and </title> tags are used to add a title to your browser's title bar. The title bar is the colored band at the top of any application that gives the name of the application.

- The <body> and </body> tags are used to surround any text that will appear in the HTML page.

All HTML documents are separated into two parts—the head and the body. Because the title is information about the document, the <title> and </title> tags are placed within the <head> and </head> tags.

> **Tip**   Many, although not all, HTML tags come in pairs. You use the first tag in the pair (for example, <html>) to tell the computer to start applying the format. The second tag (for example, </html>) requires a slash in front of the tag name that indicates to the computer to stop applying the format. The first tag usually is referred to by the name within the bracket (such as HTML). You can refer to the second tag as the end, or close, tag (such as end HTML).

One More Page

If you were to create another simple Web page, you would see that the same four HTML tags are present in this document. Only the text that appears between each pair of tags is changed.

```
<html>
<head><title>My Second Web Page</title></head>
<body>
This is my second Web page.
</body>
</html>
```

Saving and Viewing an HTML Page

In order to view your own page in a browser, you first must save it. Because you've created an HTML document, you will want to save your file with an .htm extension (first.htm, for example) so that you recognize it quickly.

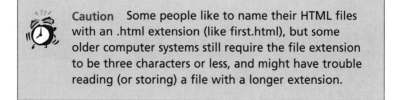

Caution   Some people like to name their HTML files with an .html extension (like first.html), but some older computer systems still require the file extension to be three characters or less, and might have trouble reading (or storing) a file with a longer extension.

You can preview any HTML file in your browser, even when that file is stored on your computer rather than on a Web server. In Internet Explorer, you can view your new file by selecting Open from the File menu. Figure 2.2 shows you how Internet Explorer displays the first.htm file that you created in Figure 2.1.

Tip   Although you don't see them, HTML commands are sitting behind the scenes of every document you open in your Web browser. You can see the HTML commands by selecting Source from the View menu of Internet Explorer (other browser may use different menu commands). When you find a page on the Web that you like, you can view the source code to learn how you can use HTML to create something similar.

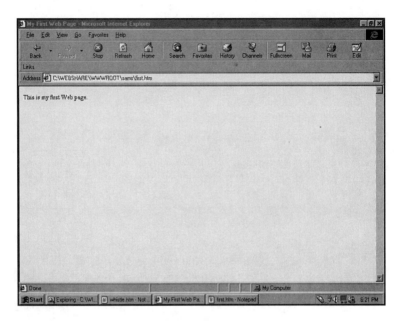

FIGURE 2.2 My First Web Page as it appears in the Internet Explorer browser. Notice that the title bar contains the text between the <title> and </title> tags and the body of the browser contains the text between the <body> and </body> tags.

> **Caution** Some Web pages use frames to display more than one HTML page at the same time (see Chapter 12, "Creating Frames"). To view the source code for this type of page, make sure you use your mouse to highlight some portion of the page you are interested in before you select Source from the View menu.

How Browsers Work

As great as Web browsers are at interpreting HTML commands, you should be aware of some limitations. Although all HTML commands are the same, not all browsers interpret the commands in the same way. Some browsers, such as Lynx, can only display text even if the HTML author added images to the document. Some older browsers do not understand the newer HTML 4 commands and may produce errors rather than text. What's more, some of the newest browsers enable the viewers to determine which window display size, fonts, and colors they prefer when viewing Web pages, even if those settings are different from what you, the Web author, want them to see.

Don't despair, there is good news. Most Web pages will look the same, or almost the same, on every browser regardless of the computer system— PC, Macintosh, or UNIX. With each lesson in this book, you'll find tips to help ensure that your pages are viewed as you intended. Keep these tips in mind as you create your own Web pages and you'll avoid the disappointment that many novice Web authors face as they realize that the page they worked so hard on looks awful on another computer or browser.

> **Tip** The Web itself offers Web page designers the opportunity to preview their pages on a number of different browsers at one time. Web sites such as the Web Site Garage (www.websitegarage.com) will show you exactly how each browser will interpret your page. You can use this information to redesign your page to help ensure that most people see your page the way you intend.

Don't Forget the Basics

As you continue through the lessons in this book, you'll discover that HTML is very forgiving. Even if you enter incorrect commands or enter the right commands in the wrong order, you'll find that most Web browsers will understand what you intended to do and interpret the page correctly. That's great for novice page authors, but if you want to move beyond the novice level, you'll need to follow some basic Web coding principles. Following is a brief list of those principles, but you'll learn more in later chapters.

- *Include all the required HTML elements that you learned in this chapter*—You might want to create a template for yourself that already includes these tags. You can use the file created in Figure 2.1 as a template. Whenever you create a new HTML document, open your template file, add your new text, and save the new file.

- *Use lowercase for all tags*—To the browser, <HEAD>, <Head>, and <head> all mean the same thing. That won't always be true. Use the same lowercase spelling for all of your commands and you won't be caught having to recode your pages when the standard changes.

- *Never use spaces in filenames*—Older computer systems have trouble reading filenames that include spaces such as *my first page.htm*. Instead, you can use a couple of file management tricks to replace the spaces. 1) Use an underscore (_) to represent spaces, like my_first_page.htm. 2) Use initial capital letters to indicate new words in a filename, such as MyFirstPage.htm.

Table 2.1 shows a list of the tags you learned in this lesson. A similar table of new HTML tags will appear at the end of other lessons.

TABLE 2.1   HTML Tags Used in This Lesson

HTML Tag	Closing	Description of Use
<html>	</html>	Surrounds all the text in an HTML file.
<head>	</head>	Contains information about the document.
<title>	</title>	Identifies the title of the page. This is used within the <HEAD> tag.
<body>	</body>	Surrounds the text of the page.

In this lesson, you've learned:

- Any text editor, including Microsoft Notepad, can be used to create Web pages, or HTML documents.

- Every HTML document must begin with the `<html>` tag and end with its pair, the `</html>` tag.

- All HTML documents are separated into two parts—the head and the body.

- All HTML tags should be typed in lowercase.

LESSON 3
Adding Text and Formatting

In this lesson, you will learn how to add paragraphs, text emphasis, and headings in your Web pages. You'll also learn how to add lines and color to your text.

Paragraphs

You might not realize it, but you already learned how to create an HTML paragraph in Chapter 2, "Creating Your First Page." In HTML, a paragraph is created whenever you insert text between the <body> tags. Look at the code from Chapter 2 again:

```
<html>
<head><title>My First Web Page</title></head>
<body>
This is my first Web page.
</body>
</html>
```

Web browsers see that you want text and they display it. Web browsers don't pay any attention to how many blank lines you put in your text; they only pay attention to the HTML commands. In the following HTML code, you'll see a new tag that's used to separate paragraphs. The <p> tag, or paragraph tag, tells the browser to add a blank line before it displays any text that follows, as shown in Figure 3.1.

```
<html>
<head><title>Typing Paragraphs in HTML</title></head>
<body>
This is the first line.
```

```
But is this the second?<P>
No, this is.
</body>
</html>
```

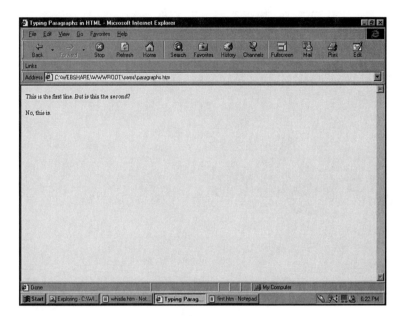

FIGURE 3.1   The browser ignores the blank line I inserted and instead puts the line break after the <p> tag.

Web browsers do something else with paragraph text that you should be aware of: they wrap the text at the end of the browser window. In other words, when the text in your Web page reaches the edge of the browser window, it automatically continues on the next line regardless of where the <p> is located.

The <p> tag always adds a blank line, but you might not always want a blank line between your text. Sometimes you just want your text to appear on the next line (such as the lines of an address or a poem). You can use another new tag, the line break, or <br> tag, as shown in Figure 3.2.

This new tag forces the browser to move any text following the tag to the next line of the browser, without adding a blank line in between. Figure 3.3 shows you how the browser uses these two tags to format your text.

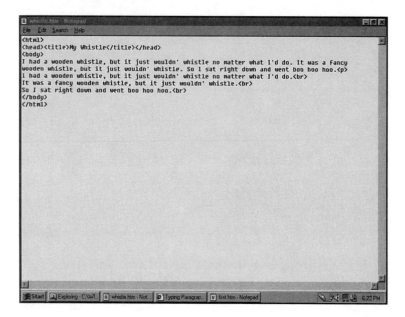

FIGURE 3.2   The <p> and <br> tags help to separate your text into lines and paragraphs.

Text Emphasis

So far you've learned how to add text, but here you will learn how to format it. You occasionally will want to add emphasis to your text to make it stand out. HTML enables you to quickly apply boldface (using the <b> or <strong> tags) and italic type (using the <i> or <em> tags).

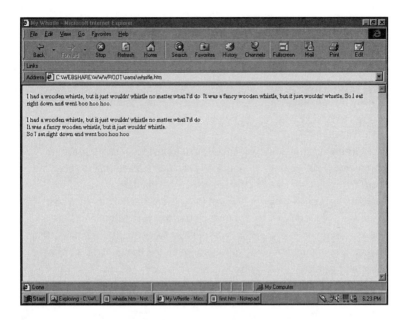

FIGURE 3.3 The browser inserts line breaks and blank paragraph separators only where you place the correct HTML tags.

Tip Why do two tags that do the same thing exist? The <b> tag tells the browser to place the text in bold-face font. The <strong> tag tells the browser to place a strong emphasis on the text. Right now, the HTML standard for strong emphasis is boldface. In later versions of HTML, that standard may change. In the year 2005, the <strong> tag might mean that your text will flash in an alternating hot pink and lime green combination. Yikes! In the same way, the <em> (emphasis) tag tells the browser to render the text in italics, the same as the <i> tag does, but it may not always be the same.

Most Web page authors use <b> and <i> because it's shorter to type and easier to remember. If you like to live on the edge, however, go ahead and use the <strong> and <em> tags.

Headings

Separating your text into paragraphs isn't the only way to format your Web pages. HTML enables you to add six different heading tags to your pages by using the tags <h1> through <h6>. These tags have an associated closing tag and are very simple to use. Look at the following line of code:

```
<h1>This is Heading 1</h1>
```

The closing heading tags also create an automatic paragraph break; in other words, all headings automatically include a blank line to separate them from the text. Heading 1, the <h1> tag, is the largest font of the heading tags and Heading 6, the <h6> tag, is the smallest. In fact, you usually will only see Web page authors use the <h1> through <h3> tags because the remaining tags, <h4> through <h6>, actually are smaller than normal text. Figure 3.4 shows a sample of all the heading tags compared to normal text.

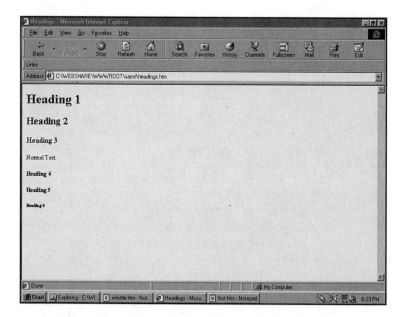

FIGURE 3.4 Notice that HTML's Heading 4 is the same size as normal text, but Headings 5 and 6 actually are smaller.

Caution Other formatting tags exist in HTML, but their use is discouraged in HTML 4 and will likely be eliminated altogether in future versions in favor of style sheets. The World Wide Web Consortium (W3C) is determined that HTML will be used to identify types of information (text, headings, tables, and so on), but will not be used to format that information.

Adding Style

The release of HTML 4 marked a change in the way Web developers apply formatting to their documents. HTML 4 introduced the concept of *style sheets* to Web developers. Style sheets enable developers to specify the fonts, colors, page margins, borders, backgrounds, and other *attributes* that allow you to add your own style to the Web pages that you create.

Style Sheets Web developers use style sheets to specify formatting instructions for a single document or group of documents.

Attribute A special code used with HTML tags that controls how the tag works.

You can create style sheets in three different ways: inline, embedded, and linked.

- **Inline** style sheets apply specific formatting styles to one HTML tag at a time. Even if you have three <h1> tags in your document, you could make each one look different by applying separate inline styles to each tag. By the same token, you could make them all look the same by applying the same inline styles to each tag.

- **Embedded** style sheets apply the same set of formatting styles to all the tags in the documents. You could specify the formatting for all the <h1> tags in your document at one time. If you later decide to change the format of the <h1> tag, you only have to change it once for each document rather than once for each tag (as in inline styles).

- **Linked** style sheets are created as a separate document. That separate document defines all the formatting styles for each tag you plan to use in all the HTML documents you are creating. You then link each HTML document to the separate style sheet document to apply the formatting. If you later decide to change the formatting of any tag, you would do it once in the style sheet document and the tag would change in each HTML document linked to that style sheet.

You learn how to create linked style sheets in Chapter 11, "Adding Your Own Style." Throughout the book, however, you'll see how inline and embedded styles can enhance your Web pages.

Tip   Even without all the formatting benefits that style sheets provide, Web developers can rejoice in knowing that using style sheets will no doubt be the biggest time saver they've ever encountered. Because you can apply style sheets to as many HTML documents as you like, making changes will take a matter of minutes rather than days.

Before style sheets, if you wanted to change the appearance of a particular tag in your Web site, you would have to open each document, find the tag you wanted to change, make the change, save the document, and continue on to the next document. With style sheets, you can change the tag in the single style sheet document and have the changes take effect immediately in all the pages linked to it.

Formatting Text with Styles

Embedded style sheets are defined between the <head> tags of an HTML document because they contain information about the entire document. In the following example, we've added some embedded style elements that set the font, font size, and font color for the body text of the basic HTML document we created in Chapter 2. In Figure 3.5, you can see how those styles change the appearance of the document in the browser.

```
<html>
<head><title>My First Web Page</title></head>
<style type="text/css">
body {font-family:"Arial";
      font-size:"12pt";
      color:red}
</style>
<body>
This is my <b><i>first</i></b> Web page.
</body>
</html>
```

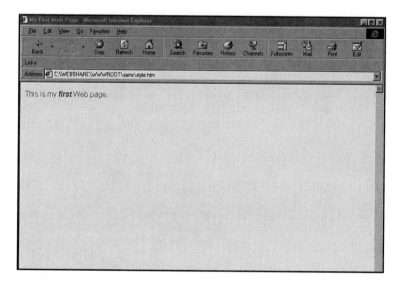

Figure 3.5 The browser applies the style attributes to the text in the <body> tags.

Don't worry, this isn't as hard as it looks. The `<style type="text/css">` indicates to the browser that you are defining a standard HTML 4 style sheet; the `</style>` tag ends the style sheet definition. In addition to the `<style>` tag, any style definition is going to include three elements: the HTML tag to which the following attributes will apply (`body`), the attribute that you are applying (`font-size`), and the format for that attribute (`12pt`).

When you are applying more than one attribute for a tag, those attributes are separated by a semicolon and enclosed in curly brackets. The specific formats for each attribute are enclosed in quotes.

> **Tip** Unless you, or the people viewing your pages, have adjusted the browser's default settings, normal HTML body text appears as 12pt Times New Roman font on most computer systems.

Table 3.1 reminds you of the formatting tags you learned in this lesson.

TABLE 3.1 HTML Tags Used in This Lesson

HTML Tag	Closing	Description of Use
`<b>`	`</b>`	Boldface text.
` `		Line break. Forces text to the next line.
`<em>`	`</em>`	Emphatic (italic) text. Usually the same as `<i>`.
`<h1>`	`</h1>`	A first-level heading.
`<h2>`	`</h2>`	A second-level heading.
`<h3>`	`</h3>`	A third-level heading.
`<h4>`	`</h4>`	A fourth-level heading. Rarely used.

HTML Tag	Closing	Description of Use
`<h5>`	`</h5>`	A fifth-level heading. Rarely used.
`<h6>`	`</h6>`	A sixth-level heading. Rarely used.
`<i>`	`</i>`	Emphatic (italic) text.
`<p>`		Paragraph break. Forces a blank line.
`<strong>`	`</strong>`	Strong (boldface) text. Same as `<b>`.
`<style>`	`</style>`	Surrounds the style attributes for a document. The standard open tag should be `<style type= "text/css">`.

In this lesson, you've learned:

- The `<p>` tag, or paragraph tag, tells the browser to add a blank line before it displays any text that follows; the `<br>` tag moves your text to the next line without adding a blank line.

- HTML enables you to add emphasis to your text with boldface (using the `<b>` tag) and italic type (using the `<i>` tag).

- Three different style sheet exist in HTML: inline, embedded, and linked. You'll learn more about style sheets in Chapter 11, "Adding Your Own Style."

LESSON 4
Creating Tables

In this lesson, you'll learn to build tables using HTML and how to control the layout and appearance of a Web page using tables.

Simple Tables

Traditionally, *tables* have been used for displaying tabular data (such as numbers) in rows and columns. The flexibility of HTML 4, however, enables Web developers to create tables that display more than just numbers. In fact, as important as the capability to display tabular data is, even more important to Web designers is the capability to control the layout of other document elements such as text and images.

 Table   An arrangement of horizontal rows and vertical columns. The intersection of a row and a column is called a *cell*.

 Caution   Although HTML tables look similar to your favorite spreadsheet, HTML tables won't perform mathematical functions.

HTML tables are not difficult to create, but they do require some organization. All HTML tables begin with the <table> tag and end with a </table> tag. In between those tags are three other tags to be aware of, as follows:

<tr> defines a horizontal row.

<td> defines a data cell within that row.

<th> specifies a data cell as a table heading. In newer browsers, a table heading cell is formatted as centered and bold.

Remember that Web browsers ignore any spaces, tabs, and blank lines that you include in your HTML document. So feel free to use spacing to help you keep track of the table tags. Figure 4.1 includes enough blank spaces between the tags so that you can see the rows and columns lining up. It makes it easier to ensure that you don't forget any tags. Figure 4.2 shows how that table looks in a browser.

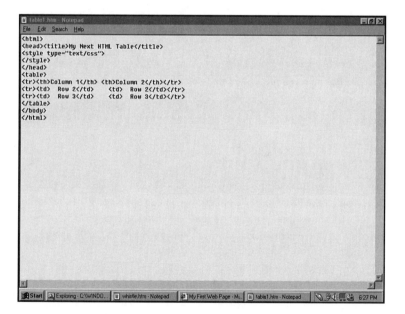

FIGURE 4.1   A simple two column, three row HTML table.

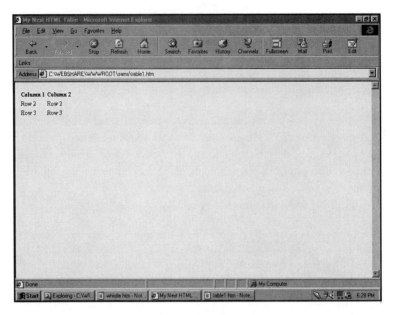

FIGURE 4.2　That same HTML table as it appears in the browser.

Formatting Tables

Now you can add some pizzazz to your simple table. In Table 4.1, you'll
see some of the different style attributes you can apply to HTML tables.
Figure 4.3 shows how you can use these attributes to create HTML table
with a little more character. Figure 4.4 shows the way the table appears in
a browser.

> **Tip**　The World Wide Web Consortium's Web site
> (www.w3.org/TR/REC-html40/struct/tables.html) has
> detailed descriptions of all the attributes available for
> tables, as well as examples of how you can use them.

TABLE 4.1 Table Style

Attribute	Default	Values
align	left	Horizontal alignment of cell contents—left, right, center, and char (which aligns around a specific character, usually a decimal or comma)
background		Background image of a table
bgcolor		Background color
border	0	Width of the border (in *pixels*—<table> tag only)
cellpadding	0	Space between border and content (in pixels—<td> tag only)
cellspacing	0	Space between cells (in pixels—<td> tag only)
colspan	1	Number of columns a cell should span (merge)
rowspan	1	Number of rows a cell should span (merge)
rules	none	Where the lines (rules) appear between cells (rows, cols, or all—<table> tag only)
valign	center	Vertical alignment of cell contents (top, bottom, or baseline)
width	*to fit*	Width of table or cells (in pixels or as a percentage of the page)

Pixel   A pixel is the size of a single dot of color on your monitor. The monitor's display resolution affects the size of a pixel. A display resolution of 800×600 means that your monitor will display 800 pixels in width by 600 pixels in height. The pixel size on a monitor that displays at a resolution of 1024×800 would be much smaller than one on a monitor with a resolution of 800×600.

A table with a width attribute fixed at 800 pixels will fill a screen that is set to 800×600 resolution, but will only fill a portion of a screen that is set to 1024×800.

```
table1a.htm - Notepad                                                    _ 回 X
File  Edit  Search  Help
<html>
<head><title>My Next HTML Table</title>
<style type="text/css">
th {color:"red";
    font-family:"arial"}
td {color:"blue";
    font-family:"tahoma"}
</style>
</head>
<table width="50%" border="1" rules=ALL>
<tr><th bgcolor="silver">Column 1</th> <th bgcolor="silver">Column 2</th></tr>
<tr><td align="center">  Row 2</td>    <td align="center">  Row 2</td></tr>
<tr><td align="center">  Row 3</td>    <td align="center">  Row 3</td></tr>
</table>
</body>
</html>
```

FIGURE 4.3   Table attributes in HTML.

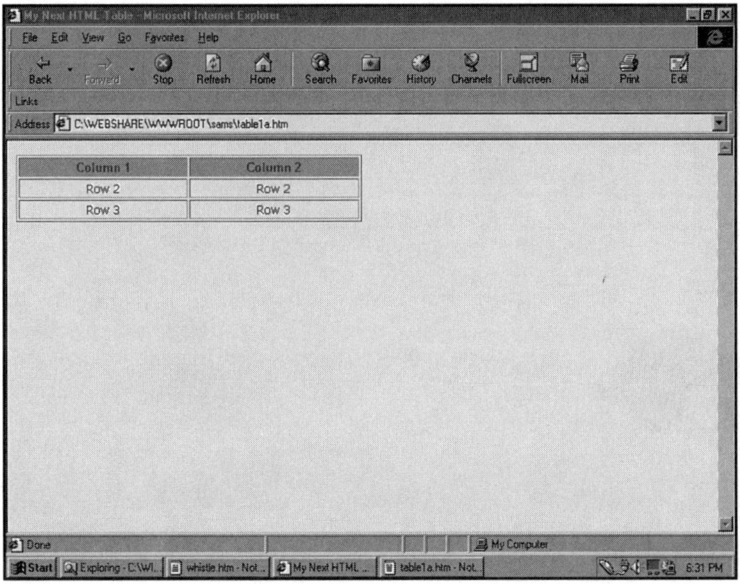

FIGURE 4.4 That same HTML table as it appears in the browser.

Advanced Tables

HTML contains two more tags that you should be aware of when formatting tables. The <colspan> and <rowspan> tags are invaluable in creating complex tables, although as you can tell from the HTML in Figure 4.5, using them makes it harder to keep your HTML document organized. Figure 4.6 shows how the table looks in a browser.

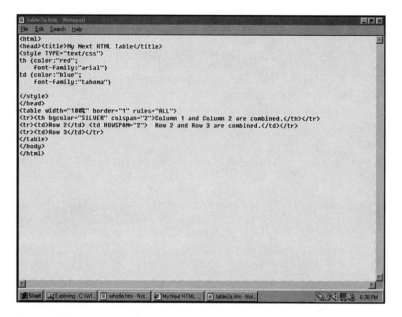

FIGURE 4.5 Using the `<colspan>` and `<rowspan>` tags to create complex tables.

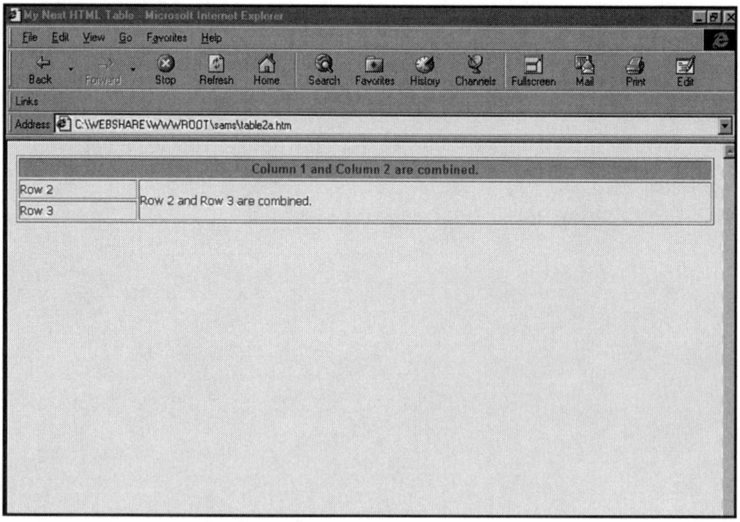

FIGURE 4.6 Figure 4.5 rendered in the browser.

Using Tables for Layout

Look at the source code of some of your favorite Web pages, and I'll bet that you'll find they were created using tables. Following are some of my favorite Web pages that contain tables:

www.yahoo.com   The columns of search categories are created with tables.

www.webdeveloper.com   This site essentially is a three column table.

www.microsoft.com   Microsoft, too, uses tables to design the layout of its Web site.

http://disney.go.com/disneyatoz/fan   Disney's Ultimate Fan site shows another creative use of tables in layout.

www.sun.com   Sun's very graphic home page is made up of a series of small images placed in table cells. Breaking up a large image into many smaller images will help the page load faster.

> **Tip**   Even if you don't plan to place a border around the cells on your table, it's much easier to see how your HTML commands are interpreted by your Web browser when you have the borders turned on—<table border="1">. After you are satisfied that the table is formatted correctly and your content is where you want it to be, you can remove the border attribute, leaving just the <table> tag.

Table 4.2 lists the HTML tags that were discussed in this lesson.

TABLE 4.2   HTML Tags Used in This Lesson

HTML Tag	Closing	Description of Use
<table>	</table>	Identifies the title of the page; used within the <head> tag.
<td>	</td>	Table data cell. Similar to a column.
<th>	</th>	Table heading.
<tr>	</tr>	Table row. Surrounds table cells <td> and headings <th>.

In this lesson, you've learned:

- Tables control the layout of HTML document elements such as text, navigation, and images.

- Extra spaces in your HTML documents help you keep track of the table tags; Web browsers ignore any spaces.

- The <colspan> and <rowspan> tags merge cells in complex tables.

LESSON 5

Linking Text and Documents

In this lesson, you'll learn how to use HTML's most valuable feature: hyperlinks.

What Is a URL?

Ask anyone and they'll tell you, far and away the feature that makes HTML so worthwhile is the capability to *hyperlink* from one place to another. All Web pages, Internet resources, files, and so on, have an address. That address is known as a *Uniform Resource Locator*, or URL. Before you can link to another page (or resource), you have to know its address. You can find the URL for any resource in the Address box (or Location box) of your browser.

 Hyperlink The text that enables you to jump from a Web document to another location.

The <a> tag (called an anchor) is used to define hyperlinks. Unlike most other HTML tags, the <a> tag *requires* an attribute. When you use the <a> tag, you must specify whether you want the enclosed text to *link to* someplace (with the <a href="the URL you want to link to"> tag) or be *linked from* someplace (with the <a name="the place in a document you want to link to"> tag). The following section provides some examples.

Hyperlinks

The easiest link to learn is the hyperlink to another location. The `<a>` tag with the `href` attribute, and its closing tag, `</a>`, surround any text that you want to highlight. The default hyperlink highlighting in HTML is underlined blue text. In the following example, you would click on the words *click here* to jump (hyperlink) to the document found at the URL inside the quotes.

```
Please <a href="http://www.microsoft.com">click here</a> to
open the Microsoft Web site.
```

Tip   Did you know that you can copy the URL of any Web page from your browser? Just highlight the address in the Address box (or Location box) and select Edit, Copy (or press Ctrl+C). Then select Edit, Paste (or press Ctrl+V) to paste the address between the quotes of the `href` attribute.

Linking to Other Files and Email

You can link to more than just other people's Web sites. You can use the same `href` attribute to link to email addresses, to other pages of your own Web site, or even to other files on your own computer. The hyperlink to point to another file (second.htm) on my own computer, for example, is shown in the following code. In this example, the second.htm file is stored in the same directory as the page linking to it.

```
Please <a href="second.htm">click here</a> to open my second
Web page.
```

If, however, my second.htm file was stored in another directory (for example, the Links directory) the hyperlink would need to include the directory name too, as in the following:

```
Please <a href="links/second.htm">click here</a> to open my
other page.
```

The href attribute changes slightly if you want to link to a file that is not part of your Web site. You'll need to tell the Web browser that the file is not located on the Web server. You can see how that is accomplished in the following example:

```
Please <a href="file:\\servername\foldername\filename.exten-
sion">click here</a> to open my favorite file.
```

If I wanted to link to my dogs.doc file in the 4legs folder of my animals server, for example, my hyperlink would look like the following:

```
Please <a href="file:\\animals\4legs\dogs.doc">click here</a>
to open my favorite file.
```

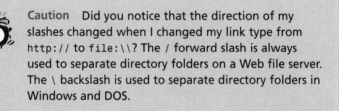

Caution Did you notice that the direction of my slashes changed when I changed my link type from `http://` to `file:\\`? The / forward slash is always used to separate directory folders on a Web file server. The \ backslash is used to separate directory folders in Windows and DOS.

You also can link to an email address by using the mailto prefix, as shown in the following code line. When you click on the words *click here*, an email window that enables you to type in your message to Mickey Mouse will appear.

```
Please <a href="mailto:mickey.mouse@disney.com">click here
</a> to send mail to Mickey.
```

Linking within the Same Page

Now that you know how to link to other resources, you might want your hyperlinks to be more meaningful. HTML enables you to use hyperlinks to point to a specific spot (anchor) in an HTML document, instead of just pointing to the entire document. An example would be if you have a list of headlines at the top of your HTML document that point to a more complete article at the bottom of your document. This is easy in HTML. Remember that anchor tags come with two attributes: href (which has already been discussed), and name.

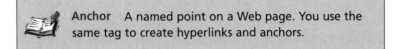

Anchor A named point on a Web page. You use the same tag to create hyperlinks and anchors.

The <a> tag also enables you to name an anchor (or bookmark) in your document with the name attribute. HTML then enables you to use the anchor tag to point directly to that bookmark. Figure 5.1 demonstrates how the example in the previous paragraph might look in HTML. Figure 5.2 shows that same document in the browser.

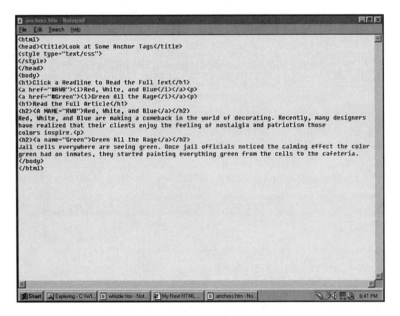

FIGURE 5.1 Notice how the *href* attribute points to the location named by the *name* attribute.

Caution The `<a href>` tag includes the same URL format you've seen before, but also includes the # symbol to separate the filename from the named anchor.

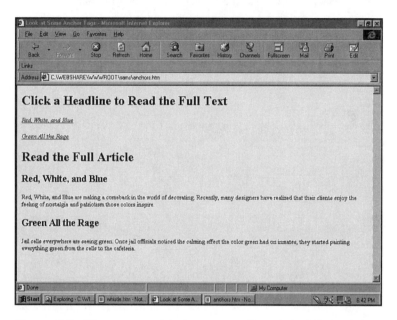

FIGURE 5.2 The `<a>` tag with the href attribute is highlighted, but the `<a>` tag with the name attribute is not.

Tip When naming anchors, remember to keep the names short and don't use spaces. These aren't HTML requirements, but following these guidelines certainly makes linking easier. Look at the example in Figure 5.1 again. The named anchor for the Red, White, and Blue article is the abbreviated RWB.

Linking to an Anchor in Another Page

Creating a hyperlink to an anchor in another page requires only one more element—the addition of the URL. As you learned before, you can link to an anchor on a file in your own Web site, as shown in Figure 5.3, or to a known anchor in a file on another Web site. The key word in that sentence is *known*. You can't link to a specific spot on a file unless that spot is already recognized, by the Web browser, as a named anchor.

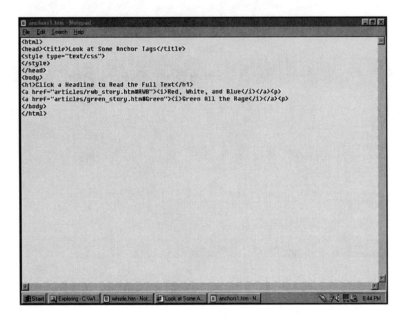

FIGURE 5.3 Notice that each `href` attribute includes a folder name (`articles`), filename (`rwb_story.htm`), and the specific anchor name (`RWB`).

> **Caution** The World Wide Web Consortium (W3C), in the new XHTML and XML standards (which will eventually replace HTML), are calling for the use of a new attribute for the `<a>` tag called `id` to replace the `name` attribute. The smart thing to do, to make sure that you comply with the new standard when it is released, would be to use both tags in your documents, as in the following example:
>
> `<a name="top" id="top">Top</a>`

Table 5.1 lists the HTML tags that were discussed in this lesson.

TABLE 5.1   HTML Tags Used in This Lesson

HTML Tag	Closing	Description of Use
`<a href="...">`	`</a>`	Surrounds text that will link to another location.
`<a name="...">`	`</a>`	Surrounds text that will be linked to.
`<a id>`	`</a>`	Same as `<a name>`, but may soon replace it.

In this lesson, you've learned:

- Anchor tags, `<a>`, come with two attributes: `href` (which will line *to* someplace), and `name` (which will link *from* someplace).

- You can copy the URL of any Web page from your browser and paste it between the quotes of the `href` attribute in your `<a>` tag.

- The same `href` attribute will link to email addresses, to other pages of your own Web site, or even to other files on your own computer.

LESSON 6
Creating Lists

In this lesson, you'll learn to use HTML to organize your text into lists.

Types of Lists

Another way to organize the text in your Web pages is with lists. In addition to the obvious benefit of enabling you to *list* items on a page, they also provide a design benefit by letting you break up long pages of ordinary paragraphs. HTML recognizes the following list types and has tags that correspond to each.

Bulleted (unordered) lists

Numbered/lettered (ordered) lists

Definition lists

> **Tip** You should use ordered lists when the items in the list must be followed in a specific order. You should use unordered lists in other instances. You generally use definition lists for terms and their definitions, but they can have other uses as well.

Bulleted (Unordered) Lists

A bullet (usually a solid circle) appears in front of each item in an unordered list. HTML automatically creates the bullet when you use the unordered list tag, `<ul>`, together with the list item, `<li>`, tag. Although the following sample HTML shows each list item as a single line of text, your list items can be as long as you want.

```
<ul><li>first item in the list</li>
<li>second item in the list</li>
<li>third item in the list</li></ul>
```

Figure 6.1 shows how the Web browser displays an ordered list and
unordered list. The figure includes list examples from many of the following sections.

When your list items are longer than a single line of text, the Web browser
will indent the second line (and any following lines) so that the text lines up.

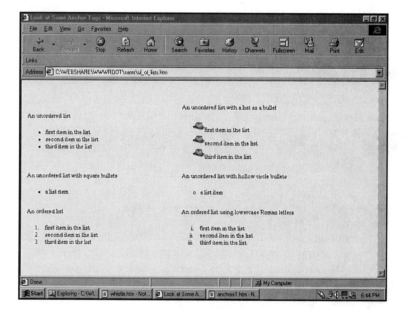

FIGURE 6.1 Ordered and unordered lists shown in the Web
browser.

Formatting Bullets

HTML automatically adds a solid circle in front of each list item as a bullet, but you have two other choices. Using style sheet tags (which you'll
learn about in Chapter 11, "Adding Your Own Style"), you can select one

of two other bullet types, a square or a hollow circle. You can see how your HTML document would look if you chose to use a square bullet instead of the standard solid circle. Figure 6.1 shows you how the Web browser displays this bullet type.

```
<html>
<head><title>Look at Some Anchor Tags</title>
<style type="text/css">
ul square {list-style-type:square}
ul hat {list-style-image:url(hat.gif)}
</style>
</head>
<body>
<ul class="square"><li>a list item</li></ul>
<p>
<ul class="hat"><li>a list item</li></ul>
</body>
</html>
```

You'll notice that this sample HTML also includes a style (list-style-image). This style will enable you to replace the plain HTML bullets for your own image. In this example, I replaced the bullets with an image of a hat. Refer to Figure 6.1 to see the results.

Numbered (Ordered) Lists

If the items in your list should follow a specific order, as in recipes or instructions, you'll want to use the ordered list tag, <ol>. With this tag, HTML automatically numbers or letters your items for you. Here's an example.

```
<ol><li>first item in the list</li>
<li>second item in the list</li>
<li>third item in the list</li></ol>
```

Notice how similar the two list samples are. Both the <ul> and <ol> tags call for the individual list items to be identified with the <li> tag. Like the <ul> tag, HTML has an automatic style for the list items within the <ol> tag. HTML will automatically number the items with the familiar Arabic numbers (1, 2, 3, and so on). What's more, it will automatically renumber the list items if you decide to add or delete items later. Once again, Figure 6.1 has an example of this type of list.

Formatting Ordered Lists

You can use style sheets for formatting ordered lists as well. In addition to the standard arabic numbers, there are four other styles that can be applied to your ordered list. Table 6.1 describes each of those types and the sample HTML below shows how you can use style sheets to create a list ordered by lowercase Roman numerals. Figure 6.1 shows an example of such a list in the Web browser.

```
<html>
<head><title>Look at Some Anchor Tags</title>
<style type="text/css">
ol.lwroman {list-style-type:lower-roman}
</style>
</head>
<body>
<ol class="lwroman"><li>a list item</li></ol>
</body>
</html>
```

TABLE 6.1   List Style Types

Sample	Style syntax	Definition
a	lower-alpha	Lowercase letters
A	upper-alpha	Uppercase letters
i	lower-roman	Small Roman numerals
I	upper-roman	Large Roman numerals

Setting a Start Value

There may be times when you'd like to start an ordered list with a number other than 1. Many times when writing instructions, you need to interrupt a numbered list with some other material, such as text or examples, and then continue the numbered list. To do this in HTML, close the first list, add the additional materials you need, and then start a new list, using the list item's value attribute to set the beginning number for the new list. Here's an example.

```
<html>
<head><title>Definition Lists</title>
<style type="text/css">
</style>
</head>
<body>
It's Payday!
<ol>
<li>Turn in your timecard.</li>
<li>Receive your paycheck.</li>
<li>Endorse your paycheck.</li>
</ol>
Congratulations! You're almost there.
<ol>
<li value="4">Put the check in the bank.</li>
</ol>
</body>
</html>
```

 Caution   The value attribute requires that you use Arabic numbering to specify the start value, even if you've chosen Roman numerals or letters for your list type.

Definition Lists

If you need it, HTML has one more type of list available to you: the definition list, which uses the <dl> tag. Rather than using the usual <li> tag to specify the items in the list, this type of list is uses the <dt> tag (for definition terms) and the <dd> tag for their definitions. Following is an example of the HTML for a definition list and Figure 6.3 shows how the Web browser formats a definition list.

```
<dl><dt>The Definition Term</dt>
<dd>Is defined below the term.</dd></dl>
```

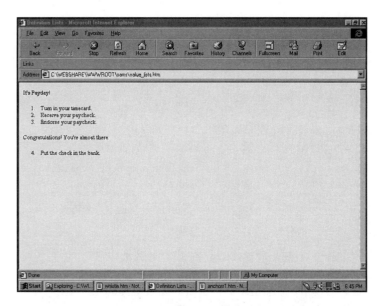

FIGURE 6.2   The Web browser shows an ordered list that was interrupted and started again using the value attribute.

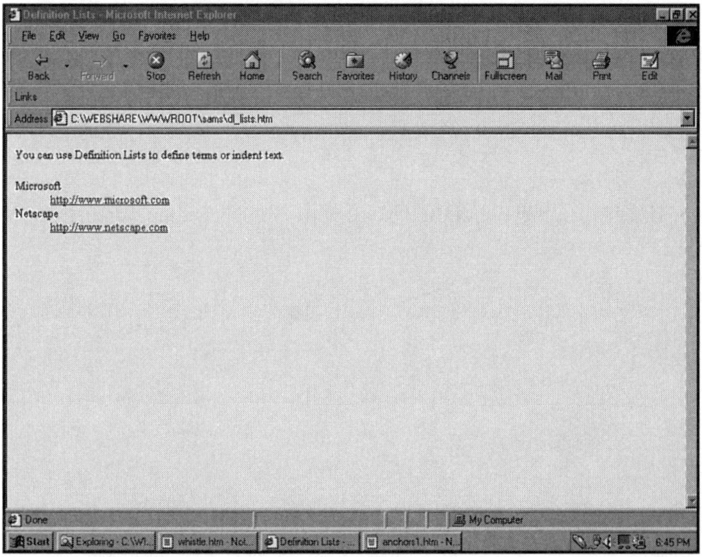

FIGURE 6.3   A definition list displayed in the browser.

Table 6.2 lists the HTML tags that were discussed in this lesson.

TABLE 6.2   HTML Tags Used in This Lesson

HTML Tag	Closing	Description of Use
<dl>	</dl>	Definition list.
<li>	</li>	List item. Used with <ol> and <ul> tags.
<dt>	</dt>	Definition term. The list item of a <dl>.
<dd>	</dd>	Definition data. Describes definition terms.
<ol>	</ol>	Ordered, or numbered/lettered, list.
<ul>	</ul>	Unordered, or bulleted, list.

In this lesson, you've learned:

- HTML recognizes three different list types: bulleted (unordered), numbered (ordered), and definition lists.

- Rather than the default bullet style (a solid circle), style sheets enable you to select two other bullet types: a square or a hollow circle.

- The value attribute of the <ol> tag sets the beginning number for your list.

LESSON 7
Adding Images

In this lesson, you'll learn how to add pizzazz to your Web pages with graphic images.

Adding Images

If the Web were nothing but text, it would still be technologically impressive, but it wouldn't be nearly as much fun. Adding images to your pages is easy; adding images that make your Web pages look professional just takes a little know-how. Luckily, you'll learn that here—and it shouldn't take longer than 10 minutes.

The two most frequently used graphics file formats found on the Web are GIF and JPEG. The *Joint Photographic Experts Group (JPEG)*, format is used primarily for realistic, photographic-quality images. The *Graphics Interface Format (GIF)*, is used for almost everything else. One new file format is gaining popularity among designers and will soon be making its presence known: the *Portable Network Graphics* format, or *PNG*, is expected to replace the GIF format someday. Don't rush out to replace all of your graphics, however; most browsers do not yet support the PNG format.

> **Tip** Sound like a pro—learn how to pronounce the graphic formats you use. GIF files are pronounced "jif" (like the peanut butter), JPEG is pronounced "jay-peg," and PNG is pronounced "ping."

Let's get down to business. You add all images by using a single HTML tag, the image source tag, `<img src="location">`. By now you probably recognize that this tag actually is an `<img>` tag with an attribute (src) and attribute value (location), but because all images require a src attribute, it's easier to refer to it as a single tag. The result of the following sample HTML appears in Figure 7.1.

```html
<html>
<head><title>My First Image</title></head>
<style type="text/css">
</style>
<body>
This is an image in my first Web page.<img
src="images\happyFace.jpg">
</body>
</html>
```

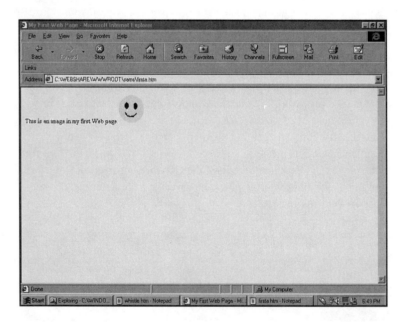

FIGURE 7.1   The `<img src>` tag inserts an image into your HTML document.

> **Caution** Be aware that the World Wide Web
> Consortium, the standards-setting body for HTML, is
> considering replacing the `<img>` tag with the more
> generic `<object>` tag. To add an image using the
> `<object>` tag, follow this format:
>
> `<object data="navbar.gif" type="image/gif"> text`
> `describing the image... </object>`

Adding Alternate Text

When browsing the Web, you might have noticed that many times when
you move your mouse pointer over an image, you see a text pop-up that
describes the image, or tells you something more about the area of the
Web site that image represents. You can see an example of that type of
text pop-up in Figure 7.2.

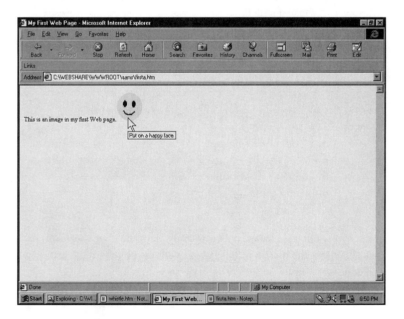

FIGURE 7.2 The `alt` attribute adds a text pop-up to your image.

The following HTML sample shows how the alt attribute is added into the <img> tag. Like the src attribute, the alt attribute tells the browser more information about the image. And, like the src attribute, you should always use the alt attribute with the <img> tag.

```
This is an image in my first Web page.<img
src="images\happyFace.jpg" alt="Put on a happy face.">
```

 alt attribute   Sets the *alternate text* for a graphic. It was named alt because it describes the text some people would see as an alternative to the image that others would see.

The alt attribute has another very important purpose. Many people with slower modem connections to the Web decide to customize their browser settings to ignore graphics because loading graphics into a Web browser can sometimes take a long time. Remember, too, that not all browsers enable you to view graphics. Some browsers, such as Lynx, have no graphics capabilities at all. The alt attribute ensures that people who can't view your graphics can still understand their context.

Tip   Although you should use the alt attribute whenever you use the <img> tag, make sure that you don't specify irrelevant text. For example, there is no point in specifying an alternate text for a decorative image (such as a bullet or a line); instead, specify an empty value (alt=" ").

Without any other attributes, the browser displays the image at its original size and aligns the bottom of the graphic with the bottom of the text. You can adjust both those settings using style sheet tags.

Image Attributes

You can use other attributes of the `<img>` tag to align the image with the text that surrounds it. Table 7.1 shows some of these attributes, and the following sections provide some examples for adding these attributes to your documents.

TABLE 7.1   Attributes Used with the `<img>` Tag

Attribute	Values	Description of Use
height	pixel or percent	Specifies the height of an image.
width	pixel or percent	Specifies the width of an image.
align	left, right, center, top, or bottom	Forces the image to align with text.

Adjusting the Height and Width

You can adjust the size of your image using the `height` and `width` attributes. You can set these attributes to a fixed pixel size or a percentage of the page size. Look at the following sample HTML lines. The first line sets the happy face image from Figure 7.1 to a fixed pixel size of 60 pixels high and 60 pixels wide. The second line sets the same image to 15 percent of the page width and 5 percent of the page height. Figure 7.3 shows how both of these look in the browser.

```
<img src="images\happyFace.jpg" alt="Put on a happy face."
height="60" width="60">
<img src="images\happyFace.jpg" alt="Put on a happy face."
height="15%" width="8%">
```

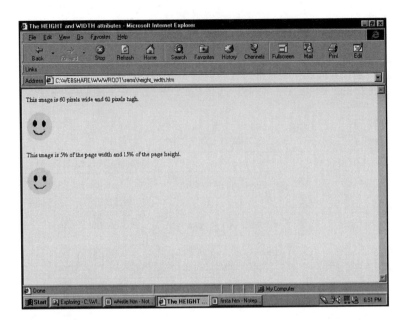

FIGURE 7.3 The height and width attributes control the size of the image.

The Web browser interprets pixels and percentages equally well when rendering an image. You need to remember, however, that your Web visitors may not use the same monitor display settings that you do. What does this mean to you? My monitor is set to 800 pixels wide. In the preceding HTML sample, I set the happy face image to 8 percent of the page width, or 64 pixels. If I viewed the same page on a monitor set to 1024 pixels wide, that 8 percent of the page width would now equal 82 pixels, which is much wider than I wanted.

If you truly want the image to be a certain percentage of the page (as you might for a graphical line), then use percentages. Using percentages ensures that the image will take up the space you want it to. If you want the image to appear a specific size, use the pixel setting.

Aligning Text and Images

You can use the `align` attribute of the `<img>` tag to force an image to appear on the left or right of a section of text. You can see an example of this attribute in action in Figure 7.4.

```
<img src="images\happyFace.jpg" alt="Put on a happy face."
height="60" width="60" align="right">
```

You also can use `align` attribute to vertically align an image with the text. The `align` attribute has three more values: `top`, `bottom`, and `center`, which are discussed in the following list. Figure 7.4 shows you a sample HTML document using the vertical alignment properties.

- Setting the `align` attribute to `top` aligns the top of the image with the top of any surrounding text.

- Setting the `align` attribute to `bottom` aligns the bottom of the image with the bottom of any surrounding text.

- Setting the `align` attribute to `center` aligns the center of the image with the center of any surrounding text.

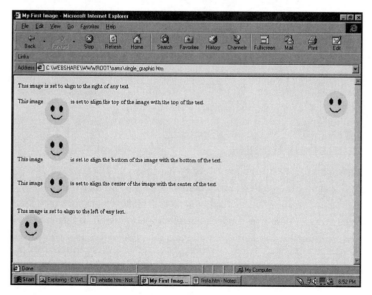

FIGURE 7.4 Notice how the `align` attribute forces the image to align with the text.

Caution   Be sure to preview your HTML documents in the browser (or in several browsers) to make sure that you are happy with how they look before you publish them. Not all browsers treat these `align` attributes in the same way.

Using Images as Links

Images are good for more than just looks. You can use them to provide creative hyperlinks to other documents. HTML makes this easy because using an image as a link is exactly the same as using text. You still are using the anchor tag (the <a> tag you learned about in Chapter 5, "Linking Text and Documents") to surround the item you want to act as the hyperlink to another document. When you link from an image, the anchor tags must surround the image tag. Following is an example of the HTML you would use:

```
<a href="DOC2.htm">
<img src="images\happyFace.jpg" alt="Click here to put on your
own happy face." height="60" width="60">
</a>
```

When the visitors move their mouse pointers over the happyFace.jpg image in this sample, they will see a pop-up that says, "Click here to put on your own happy face." When the visitors click on the image, they will open the DOC2.htm file referenced by the anchor tag.

Thumbnail Images

Another popular use of the hyperlinking capability of HTML is to link from one image to another. Why would you want to do that? Well, many times the image you want to display is so large that it takes longer to load into the browser than you think people would like to wait. If that's so, you can create a smaller version of the file, called a *thumbnail*, that will load more quickly into the browser. The visitor simply clicks the thumbnail if he wants to open the larger file. Here's how it's done.

```
<a href="large_image.jpg">
<img src="thumbnail.jpg" alt="Click here to view a larger
image." height="60" width="60">
</a>
```

As you can see, the thumbnail.jpg image will open another image (large_image.jpg). The alt attribute in this sample tells the visitor how to open the larger image.

> **Tip** Many image editor programs provide tools to help you create thumbnail images of your large graphics. You can also use standalone products, such as Cerious Software's Thumbs Plus available at http://cws.internet.com/redir/ftp://ftp.cerious.com/pub/cerious/thmpls32.exe.

Image Etiquette

Images are fun and colorful and easy to add to your HTML, but following are some etiquette rules to follow if you want your visitors to be happy with your site.

- The larger an image's file size, the longer it will take to load into the browser. Because most visitors to the World Wide Web use a slow speed modem to connect, their time is precious. If you remember that and make sure to use small images whenever possible, you'll find that your visitors are happier.

- Not only is the file size of the individual image important, but also is the total file size of your HTML document. The more images you add—even small images—the larger your file size will become. Previewing your page in several browsers will help you determine how long your page will take to load in the browser. If you find the time too slow, so will your visitors.

- While the `alt` attribute is one of the most important attributes (because it should be used every time you use the `<img>` tag), it pays to remember some simple guidelines. Make sure that the text for the `alt` attribute is relevant to the image—anything less will frustrate your visitors.

- On the subject of relevance: be sure that your images are relevant to the text. An image of an airplane works great if you're talking about travel plans, but means nothing if you are talking about wildlife.

- You can find images all over the Internet and saving them to your own computer for use later is easy (see the following tip). Just as in the publishing world, however, graphic designers can protect their images by copyright. If you've found an image you like on a commercial Web site, look for a copyright notice or other legal statement that indicate whether the image is free for the taking. There are plenty of free images available on the Internet without using copyrighted material.

> **Tip** You can copy any Web image to your own computer, as long as it isn't protected by copyright. Just right-click on the image (or hold down the mouse button if you are on a Macintosh computer) and select Save Image As from the pop-up menu. Save the file on your own computer and use it as you would any other image file.

Table 7.2 lists the HTML tags that were discussed in this lesson.

TABLE 7.2   HTML Tags Used in This Lesson

HTML Tag	Closing	Description of Use
`<img src=" ">`		Adds an image to an HTML document.
`<object>`	`</object>`	Adds an object (can be used for images) to a HTML document.

In this lesson, you've learned:

- The two most frequently used graphics file formats found on the Web are GIF and JPEG. JPEG is used primarily for realistic, photographic-quality images; GIF is used for almost everything else.

- All images are added to HTML documents with the image tag and the source attribute, `<img src="location">`.

- You can use the `<a>` tag to link an image to another document.

- Images are part of the fun of Web pages, but they are also part of the problem; large file sizes mean longer page load times.

LESSON 8

Mapping Images

In this lesson, you'll learn how to use image maps to link one image to many pages.

What Are Image Maps?

You've learned how to use an image to link to another page, but did you know that you can subdivide a single image and link each part of that image to another page? This type of subdivided image is called an *image map*.

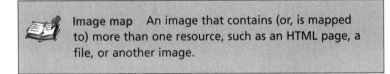

> **Image map** An image that contains (or, is mapped to) more than one resource, such as an HTML page, a file, or another image.

You've probably seen image maps on the Web, even if you didn't know what they were. Rather than creating a different image for each button in the navigation bar, many Web designers create a single image that contains all the buttons and then use image maps to link each button to the appropriate page. Look at the following examples:

- Although Northwest Airlines' Web site (www.nwa.com) uses several images on the main page, their Site Contents navigation bar is created using a single image and an image map.

- The Amazon Web site (www.amazon.com) also uses image maps to create their navigation bar.

- The navigation bar on the CDnow Web site (www.cdnow.com) also is created using an image map.

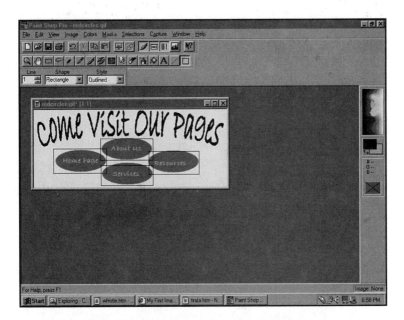

FIGURE 8.1 This image has been subdivided into four parts (one for each button on my navigation bar). Notice that some pieces of the image will not be linked to anything. Do not draw the boxes on your own image; I did it for demonstration.

Finding the Coordinates

Like any other map, image maps have coordinates. In an image map, the coordinates, which are written as pixels, mark the corners of the piece of the image that will be linked to a specific URL. Before you can create any image map, you have to know the coordinates for your image.

Many expensive programs are available that can help you determine these coordinates and give them to you in a file so that you can cut and paste them into your HTML document, but it's just as easy (and a lot less expensive) to let your image program find the coordinates and then you can just write them down on a piece of paper. Figure 8.2 shows you how Paint Shop Pro displays the coordinates for an image. I highlighted the portion of my navigation bar that I want to map to my home page and Paint Shop Pro told me which coordinates to use. As the figure shows, the highlighted section is a rectangle with corners at 47, 84 and 158, 131.

> ⏰ **Caution** You can divide your image into rectangular, circular, or irregular polygon shapes. The rectangle is the easiest shape to use when you're getting started and that's the shape used in Figure 8.2.

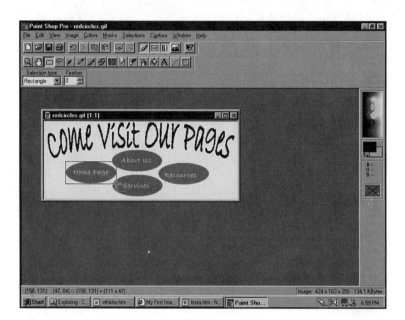

FIGURE 8.2 Paint Shop Pro displays the coordinates of a selected region of the image in the lower-left corner.

> ⏰ **Caution** The pixel coordinates for an image mark the corners of the portion of the image you are highlighting. The coordinates are relative to the entire image, not the position of the image on the Web page. Use your image editor to gather the coordinates and you won't get confused.

Client-Side Versus Server-Side

With HTML, you can create images maps that work on the client-side and the server-side. The following list indicates the differences:

- *Client-side*—When you click on a client-side image map, the Web browser does all the work to bring you to the new location. The browser selects a link that was specified for the activated region and follows it.

- *Server-side*—When you click on a server-side image map, the server the stores the Web page, interprets the commands, and brings you to the page to which you are linked.

So how do you know which one to use? Most Web page authors use only client-side image maps because they are faster, and anyone with a version 3.0 browser or higher can view client-side image maps. You could always provide text links for older browsers that don't recognize the client-side image maps. Because client-side image mapping is the type of image map used most often, it is the one you'll learn about in the following section.

> **Tip** When you are planning your Web page design, remember that you might not need to use an image map at all. You can place several smaller images close together for the same look. As long as the areas you want to link are primarily rectangular, this process is very easy with HTML and the <img> tag you learned in Chapter 7, "Adding Images."

Creating Client-Side Image Maps

Let's get started. After you have an image and have determined the coordinates for each piece of the image, you can begin mapping your image in HTML. The following HTML sample shows the image map I created for the navigation bar shown in Figure 8.1.

```
<html>
<head>
<title>Image Maps</title>
</head>
<body>
<p align="center">
<map name="NavBar">
<area shape="rect" coords="270, 91, 416, 138"
href="services.htm">
<area shape="rect" coords="139, 117, 287, 166"
href="resources.htm">
<area shape="rect" coords ="139, 61, 290, 111"
href="about.htm">
<area shape="rect" coords ="5, 84, 157, 139"
href="default.htm">
</map>
<img src="redcircles.jpg" width="424" height="166" alt="My Nav
Bar" border="0" usemap="#NavBar">
</body>
</html>
```

Look at the following HTML example for image maps a little closer:

- `<map name="x">`   Every image map needs a name. It works just like the named anchor tag `<a name>` you saw in Chapter 5, "Linking Text and Documents." It identifies the section of the HTML document that you want to reference from your image.

- `<area shape="x" coords="y" href="z">`   An `<area>` tag is required for each portion of an image that will be linked. It identifies the shape of that portion, the coordinates for it, and the URL to which it will lead.

- `</map>`   This tag closes the preceding `<map name>` tag.

- `usemap="#Map Name"`   usemap is an attribute of the `<img>` tag. It points the Web browser to the correct image map for this image. Notice the # sign that precedes the map name; it works just like creating a hyperlink to a named anchor.

The Web browser sees the image map and knows that the image will be linked. In Figure 8.3, you can see that the mouse pointer changes into a hand when your mouse hovers over a portion of the image that is mapped (as it does when placed over any other hyperlink).

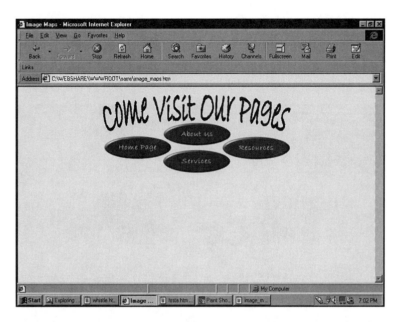

Figure 8.3 The image from Figure 8.2 displayed in the Web browser. Notice that the mouse pointer changes when it hovers over a mapped portion of the image.

Adding Text Links for Older Browsers

Because client-side image maps can only be interpreted by version 3.0 or later Web browsers, you'll need to provide another way for your visitors to get to the other pages in your Web site. The easiest way to do this is to provide text links under your image, as shown in the following HTML sample and Figure 8.4.

```
<p align="center">
<img src="redcircles.jpg" width="424" height="166" alt="My Nav
Bar" usemap="#NavBar">
<p align="center">
<a href="default.htm">Home Page</a> ¦
<a href="about.htm">About Us</a> ¦
<a href="resources.htm">Resources</a> ¦
<a href="services.htm">Services</a>
```

As you can see, text links are standard HTML `<a href>` links. They will follow the `<img>` tag and direct the viewer to the same pages they could reach with the image map. Figure 8.4 shows you how these links will look in the Web browser.

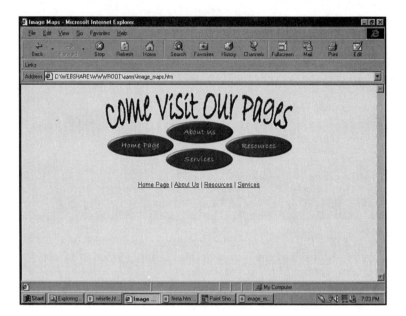

FIGURE 8.4   The image from Figure 8.2 displayed in the Web browser, with additional text links provided for older browsers.

Creating a Separate Map File

If you find it easier to keep track of a separate file, you also could create your image map in a separate file that includes all the image maps for all your pages. In the following example, I created a separate file, called map.htm:

```
<html>
<head>
<title>Image Maps</title>
```

```
</head>
<body>
<map name="NavBar">
<area shape="rect" coords="270, 91, 416, 138"
href="services.htm">
<area shape="rect" coords="139, 117, 287, 166"
href="resources.htm">
<area shape="rect" coords="139, 61, 290, 111"
href="about.htm">
<area shape="rect" coords="5, 84, 157, 139"
href="default.htm">
</map>
</body>
</html>
```

Notice that this file includes all of the information associated with the image map we created in the previous examples (everything between the <map name> and </map> tags), but it does not include an <img> tag. The <img> tag (with a usemap attribute that points to my image map file) would be included in my Web page, as shown in the following sample.

```
<html>
<head>
<title>My Web Page</title>
</head>
<body>
<p align="center">
<img src="redcircles.jpg" width="424" height="166" alt="My Nav
Bar" border="0" usemap="map.htm/#NavBar">
</body>
</html>
```

In the preceding Web page sample, the usemap attribute of the <img> tag now includes the name of the file that holds the NavBar image map (map.htm).

Table 8.1 lists the HTML tags that were discussed in this lesson.

TABLE 8.1   HTML Tags Used in This Lesson

HTML Tag	Closing	Description of Use
`<area>`		Identifies the shape (`circle`, `rect`, or `poly`), coordinates (in pixels), and URL for each section of the image.
`<map name>`	`</map>`	Surrounds the image map and gives a reference name to be used with the `usemap` attribute.
`<usemap="#map name>`		An attribute of the `<img>` tag, `usemap` points to the image map for this image.

In this lesson, you've learned:

- Image maps link a single image to multiple Internet resources. The most popular examples of image maps on the Web are for navigation bars.

- Paint Shop Pro and other graphics programs enable you to create your image *and* determine the coordinates for the image map.

- Image maps can be contained within your HTML document or in a separate file.

LESSON 9
Even More Tags

In this lesson, you'll how to use HTML to create lines, mathematical notations, and special characters such as ampersands. You'll also learn how to add information about your Web page.

Lines

A *horizontal line*, or *horizontal rule* as it is named in HTML, is one of the easiest tags to use. You can insert the <hr> tag anywhere in your document to insert a horizontal line that extends across the space allowed.

Take a look at the following sample HTML. It shows three <hr> tags: two used as a section break between text and the other used inside a table cell. Figure 9.1 shows you how they will appear in the browser.

```
<html>
<head><title>Horizontal Lines</title></head>
<style type="text/css">
td {text-align=center}
</style>
<body>
This is a horizontal line.
<hr>
<p>
This is another horizontal line.
<hr>
<p>
<table width="50%" rules=cols>
  <tr>
    <td>This is also a<hr>horizontal line.</td>
    <td>There is <br>no line on this<br>side of the table.</td>
  </tr>
</table>
</body>
</html>
```

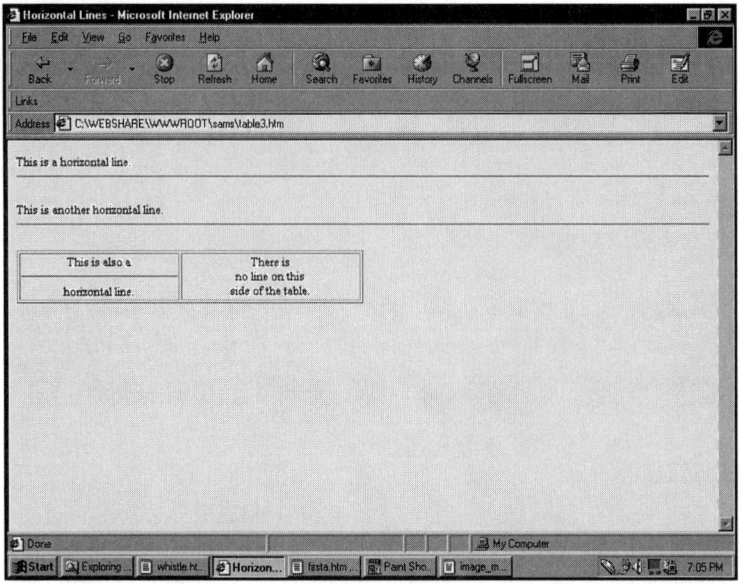

FIGURE 9.1   The <hr> tag inserts a horizontal line that stretches across the available horizontal space.

Adding Style

As with other HTML tags, you can use style sheet properties to design your own horizontal rules. You can set the height, width, and color of the line to match the design of your Web page. You learn more about style sheets in Chapter 11, "Adding Your Own Style," but for now, you will see how you can style your lines. The following HTML sample shows two different styles attached to the <hr> tag. If I use the hr.red style, I will see a red line that takes up 50 percent of the horizontal space. If I use the hr.purple style, I will see a purple line that is 4 pixels high and takes up 75 percent of the horizontal space.

```
<style type="text/css">
hr.red {color:red;
        width:50%}
hr.purple {color:purple;
            height:4;
            width:75%}
</style>
```

I've used both of those styles in the following sample HTML. Figure 9.2 shows you how those examples look in the browser.

```
<html>
<head><title>Horizontal Lines</title></head>
<style type="text/css">
td {text-align=center}
hr.red {color:red;
        width:50%}
hr.purple {color:purple;
            height:4;
            width:75%}
</style>
<body>
This is a plain horizontal line.
<hr>
<p>
This is a purple horizontal line.
<hr class="purple">
<p>
<table width="50%" rules=cols>
  <tr>
   <td>This is a red <hr class="red">horizontal line.</td>
   <td>There is <br>no line on this<br>side of the table.</td>
  </tr>
</table>
</body>
</html>
```

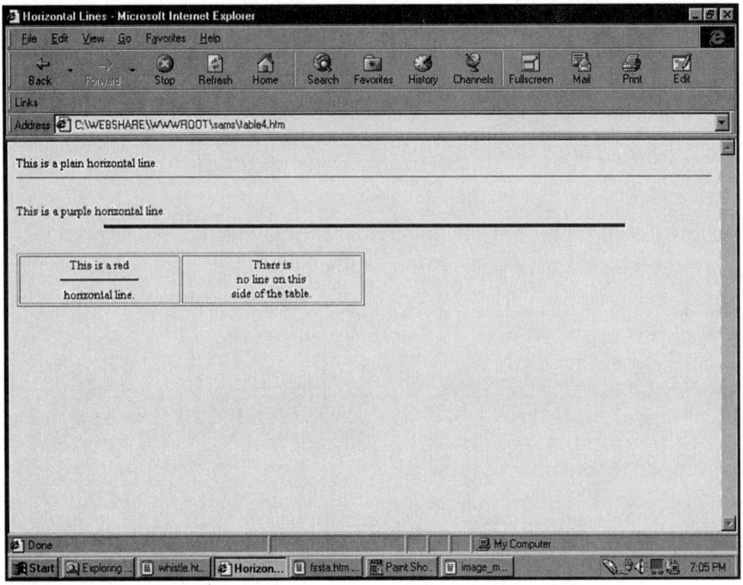

FIGURE 9.2   Applying styles to the <hr> tag changes the appearance of the line.

Special Characters

You may find that you sometimes need to use symbols on your Web pages. Symbols such as +, -, %, and & are used frequently in our everyday writing and it's easy to understand that they would appear on the Web as well. Unfortunately, not all Web browsers will display these symbols correctly. HTML uses a little computer shorthand to tell the browser how to interpret these symbols. Table 9.1 shows you some of the most frequently used codes.

TABLE 9.1   Special Character Codes

Char	Code	Description
&	&	ampersand
<	<	less than
>	>	greater than
©	©	copyright
®	®	registered trademark
±	&plusmin;	plus or minus
^{2}	²	superscript 2
^{3}	³	superscript 3
´	´	acute accent
`	`	grave accent
#	#	number sign
%	%	percent sign

The W3C's Web site (www.w3.org/TR/REC-html40/sgml/ entities.html#h-24.2.1) contains a complete list of the characters supported by HTML. You can see how many of these symbols are easy to understand: & for ampersand and > for the greater than symbol. Some of characters, such as the # and % symbols, require that you memorize number codes. Yuck. The best thing you can do is to make sure that you preview your Web pages in a variety of browsers before you publish it.

> **Tip**   Here's a special character you should remember: . The symbol stands for *non-breaking space* and is used to insert a space inside an HTML document. Because HTML ignores extra spaces between words or tags, you need to have a way to include an extra space. You can do that with the   character.

Math and Science Notations

Although HTML was first designed and used by scientists, it has yet to support mathematical and scientific notation with any degree of complexity. HTML does give you two tags to help you write simple equations. Together with the codes for special characters, the <sub> (subscript) and <sup> (superscript) tags go a long way toward creating equations, as shown in Table 9.2.

TABLE 9.2   <sup> and <sub> Tags

You Type	The Browser Displays
A² + B² </sup> = C²	$A^2 + B^2 = C^2$
CO₂ = Carbon Dioxide	CO_2 = Carbon Dioxide

If you are looking to write more complex equations, you'll need to be a little more creative. The obvious answer is to write your equation in the program you usually use and then use a graphics program to turn it into an image. You can insert that image into any HTML page, as you've already learned. That works, but the solution is limited. Because the equation is graphical, you won't be able to index or search for text within the equation. That's a big drawback, but so is the fact that images will slow down your page's load time, and your equation will not be able to be viewed by non-graphical Web browsers.

The W3C has been working on a mathematical language (MathML—Mathematical Markup Language) since 1989. MathML is similar to HTML, but hasn't been as widely used yet.

 Tip   Some commercial products are available to perform this same task. You can see a list of them on the W3C's Web site (www.w3.org/Math/).

English Isn't the Only Language

You can use HTML even if you don't write in English. URLs, hyperlinks, HTML tags, and document formatting elements are language-neutral, but text requires a specification all its own. If you write in standard U.S. English, you don't need to make any changes to the way you create your HTML documents. If you are writing text in any other language, you should specify the language for the browser. The following HTML samples show the designations for British English and French.

```
<html lang="en-br">
```

and

```
<html lang="fr">
```

The language attribute (lang) supports the same values as ISO, the International Standards Organization. You can see the full list of supported languages and their codes at www.oasis-open.org/cover/iso639-2a.html.

Text Direction

Not all languages flow from left to right like English. Some, like Hebrew, flow from right to left. You can use the dir attribute with the lang attribute to set the text direction. The dir attribute accepts two values: rtl (right to left) or ltr (left to right). Because ltr is assumed, it is not necessary to specify it unless you want to. The following example sets the language to Hebrew and the text direction to right to left.

```
<html lang="he" dir=rtl>
```

Mixing Languages in a Single Page

While the preceding example shows the lang attribute used as part of the
<html> tag at the top of your document, it's possible that you would want
to include text of one language within a document of another language;
for example, a paragraph of French within a document of English. You
can assign the lang attribute to the <p> tag to solve this problem. Look at
the following sample:

```
<html lang="en-US">
<head><title>Multi-Language Document</title></head>
<style type="text/css">
</style>
<body>
    insert your English text here.
<p lang="fr">
    mettez votre texte français ici.
<p lang="en-US">
    insert the rest of your English text here.
</body>
</html>
```

Meta Tags

Finally, you get to do something with the <head> tag. Throughout the
chapters so far, you've only seen the <title> tag used to give information
about the document; however, you can do a lot more with the <head> tag.
What's more, aside from the <title> tag, meta information doesn't usually appear in your document. You can use the meta information tag,
<meta> to identify the page's author, keywords used for searching, or a
brief description to appear in search results. You also can use the <meta>
tag to give commands to the browser. You can use as many <meta> tags as
you like in your page. You'll learn how in the sections that follow.

Improve Searching

Search engines, as you'll find in Chapter 18, "XML and the Future of the
Internet," add the content of your Web pages to their indexes. When a
potential visitor enters a search phrase, the search engine checks its index
to find that word and returns any pages that include that word. It works

great. But, what if you were a realtor and you worked hard at creating a Web page that included the words houses, housing, sale, and buy, but didn't include the words real estate. If that was the word your visitor was looking for, they would never find your page.

You can use the <meta> tag to include product names, geographic locations, industry terms, and synonyms that people might be searching for. There are three <meta> tags that work to help improve your chances of being found by a search engine:

- *Keywords*—Keywords are words that you feel people might use to search for your Web page, or synonyms for words in your document.

- *Description*—This usually is a paragraph of information about your page. Some search engines use this description to describe your page; other search engines use the first few lines of text in your document.

- *Author*—This is your opportunity to shine. Just in case someone is searching for your name, they will find it if you enter that information into the <meta> tag.

Meta information for search engines comes in pairs: name and contents. The following sample HTML includes meta information pairs for each of the preceding <meta> tags. Remember, the <meta> tags always appear between the <head> tags.

```
<html lang="en-US">
<head>
<title>Your HTML Page</title>
<meta name="keywords" contents="keywords that people like use
to search for your page.">
<meta name="description" contents="a brief paragraph describ-
ing your document.">
<meta name="author" contents="your name">
</head>
<style type="text/css">
</style>
<body>
     insert your document here.
</body>
</html>
```

Refresh and Redirect

There may be times when you want to replace one page with another, or redirect a link. You might, for example, choose to include a *splash page* on your Web site. You can use the meta information to force the page to change within a given time span.

 Splash page   The introductory page used by some Web page authors to show flashy graphics or a product logo before continuing on to the rest of the site's contents.

You also can use the `refresh` tag, shown in the following code, to refresh the same page. If you have a page that you update frequently and want to make sure that people always see the most recent version, you can enter the page's own URL in the `refresh` tag. When the browser sees the `refresh` tag, it will present the requested URL in the specified time.

```
<meta http-equiv="refresh" content="time in seconds, URL for
new page">
```

Caution   Because not all Web browsers support this attribute, authors should include some content on the splash page to enable users to move to the next page on their own if their browser doesn't support this tag.

Expiration Dates

If you have a page that you change frequently, you can specify an expiration date in the `<meta>` tag to ensure that the Web browser will look for a newer version, rather than display an older version that may still be stored in the browser's memory. Look at the example that follows.

```
<meta http-equiv="expires" contents="Sun, 11 July 1999
00:00:00 GMT">
```

When you enter the URL for this page in your browser, it will check its history files to see whether a copy is stored there. If so, it will check the meta information to see whether this page is still valid. If the expiration date has passed, the browser will look to the Web for a more recent copy before displaying the page.

Table 9.3 lists the HTML tags that were discussed in this lesson.

TABLE 9.3   HTML Tags Used in This Lesson

HTML Tag	Closing	Description of Use
`<hr>`		Inserts a horizontal rule (line) in a page.
`<meta>`		Identifies information about the document.
`<sub>`	`</sub>`	Surrounds subscripted text.
`<sup>`	`</sup>`	Surrounds superscripted text.

In this lesson, you've learned:

- The `<hr>` tag will add a horizontal line to your HTML document. Use style sheet properties to adjust the color, width, and height.

- Symbols such as +, -, and % require a little computer shorthand to tell the browser how to interpret these symbols. This shorthand begins with an ampersand (&) and ends with a semicolon (;).

- Add other languages to your HTML documents by using the lang attribute on the `<html>` tag and changing the text direction with the `dir` attribute.

- Meta information for search engines comes in pairs: name and contents, and the `<meta>` tags always appear between the `<head>` tags.

LESSON 10
Designing with HTML

In this lesson, you'll learn some designer tricks of the trade to make your pages look as good as they work.

Design Basics

Web design may have had its roots in traditional paper design, but online design is different. One of the biggest differences when designing for online is the capability to *hyperlink*. Adding hyperlinks in your Web pages gives you the capability to quickly direct your viewers to the information you want them to see, including reference material on, or off, your Web site. Unfortunately, the capability to hyperlink also is one of the biggest disadvantages to online design. Occasionally, viewers get so caught up in clicking on all those "for additional information click here" links that they forget what they were looking for in the first place; in effect, they get lost in cyberspace.

To help their users recognize which Web pages are part of the same Web site, Web site designers have a number of design elements available to them to help set the mood for their Web site. The layout, images, navigation buttons, bullets, lines, colors, and even the fonts you choose should support the overall design theme of your site. In the following sections, you'll learn how each of these elements work together. In Chapter 11, "Adding Your Own Style," you'll learn how you can use style sheets to implement these elements into your Web pages.

To design an effective Web page, you'll need to be aware of the differences in moving from traditional design to online design. Table 10.1 summarizes some of the differences. Knowing the problems you'll face is only half the battle; the rest is knowing how to avoid them. You'll learn that in the sections that follow.

TABLE 10.1 Paper Design Versus Online Design

Paper Design	Online Design
Viewers follow content along a linear path with a beginning, middle, and an end.	Using search tools, or hyperlinks, viewers can access the content at any point. Theonly way for you to controlthat movement is to provide hyperlinks and navigation.
Viewers can see an entire page (text and graphics) at the same time.	With larger graphics (or non-graphical browsers), viewers often have time to read the entire text before they ever see any images.
Serif fonts (such as Times Roman) usually are used for content; sans-serif fonts (such as Arial) usually are used for headings.	Sans-serif fonts usually are used for content; serif fonts usually are used for headings.
Viewers see an entire page (or multiple pages in a book or magazine layout). The size of the page, and the amount of content presented on it, is controlled by you, the author.	Viewers see only the amount of content that will fit on their monitor at one time, which often is only a couple of paragraphs of text. The viewer controls the presentation of the content with the size of their monitor and the browser settings.

Two whole fields of study, Information Design and Usability, are devoted to finding the most effective methods of communicating your message. Researchers in these fields have come up with some standard design guidelines that can help you make the most of the material you have to present. Following are some facts I'll bet you didn't know:

- Red, yellow, and green are the most difficult colors of text to read online. It's best not to use them or to use them sparingly. You'll learn more about colors and fonts in the subsequent sections.

- Your visitors read almost 50 percent slower online than on paper. You can counteract that by keeping your page length short (no more than two to three screen lengths) and providing tables and bulleted lists to give their eyes a rest from large blocks of text.

- Animated images and moving text catch the eye of potential visitors, but most people find them annoying if they continue to move while the visitor is trying to read or search for content on the page. You'll learn about these features in Chapter 14, "Creating Active Web Pages."

- If your visitors are looking for a particular piece of information, they will search your site for less than a minute before moving on to some other site, unless they are confident that you have the information they are looking for. A well-designed Web site will help your visitors find their information quickly. You'll learn how in the "Layout, Content, and Navigation" section.

Layout, Content, and Navigation

Because people tend to read online text more slowly than paper text, Web site designers use *page layout* techniques to help make content more readable.

Page layout   The arrangement of text, graphics, and *whitespace* on a page.

Whitespace   Refers to the background of a page. Note that this space does not have to be white.

In general, when designing a Web site, you will need to keep the following key tips in mind. Figure 10.1 shows you how some of these layout tricks work to emphasize your content.

- *Keep paragraphs short and include a margin*—Keep your paragraphs under ten lines and include a margin. If you want viewers to read your text, you'll need to make it easy for them. You'll find out how to add margins when you learn about style sheets in Chapter 11.

- *Break up long sections of text with bullets, tables, and headings*—Information design research has shown that online readers scan text, rather than read it, until they find what they're looking for. Bullets and headings help users find things more quickly.

- *Keep pages no longer than three screen lengths*—Don't put all the content of your entire site on one page. In general, use one page for each topic. If a topic is so involved that it requires more than three screen lengths to discuss, put it on more than one page.

- *Don't underline any text unless it is a hyperlink*—Online viewers expect anything underlined to be clickable. If you use underlining for another purpose, such as formatting your headings, you will confuse your readers.

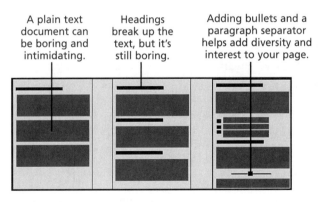

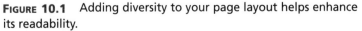

FIGURE 10.1   Adding diversity to your page layout helps enhance its readability.

If your Web site contains more than one page, you'll want to include some way for your visitors to find the other pages in your site. A good navigation system is more than a table of contents; it is a defined structure for the site that gives your visitors information about your site. Your navigation system can consist of text links or image links (refer to Chapter 7, "Adding Images"). Whichever link type you choose, your navigation system should appear on every page of your site to help orient your users.

> **Tip** Many designers use *frames* as a navigation tool. A frame is a portion of your HTML document that displays a separate HTML. You'll learn how to create frames, and use them effectively, in Chapter 12, "Creating Frames."

Fonts and Colors

Color is an exciting way to add interest to your Web pages. In addition to the obvious splash of color that images provide, you can add color to your fonts and page backgrounds. Be creative in your choices, but use a critical eye to review the results. Some colors are very difficult to read online and some color combinations are nearly impossible to decipher. Always provide some contrast in your color choice: use a light-colored font on a dark background and a dark-colored font on a light background.

> **Tip** In HTML, colors are defined by name (such as navy, red, and black), or by a hexadecimal number. The six-digit number represents the amount of RGB (red, green, and blue) in the color. To see a list of colors and their numerical equivalent, check out these Web sites:
>
> `http://www.onr.com/user/lights/colclick.html` or `http://www.hidaho.com/colorcenter/cc.html`.

So, how do you add color? With style sheet properties, of course. HTML does have a <font> tag that enables you to specify a font (such as Arial or Times Roman) and colors and sizes, but according to the W3C, users are not supposed to use it. Instead, they've given you the font-family, font-size, color, and background properties for your style sheets. The following code provides an example of how you can specify your fonts for the <body> and <h1> tags.

 **Caution** Just because you can specify a font doesn't mean that your visitor will have that font on his or her computer. To be on the safe side, always specify at least one alternate font, as I did in the following example. All but the most basic computers will have Arial and Times New Roman, so it's not a bad idea to use one of those two as your alternate font.

```html
<html>
<head><title>Fonts and Colors</title></head>
<style type="text/css">
body {font-family:Trebuchet MS, Arial;
      color:navy;
      font-size:12;
      background:white}
h1    {font-family:Bookman Old Style, Times New Roman;
      color:white;
      font-size:14;
      background:navy}
</style>
<body>
<h1>Fonts and Colors</h1>
This text is navy on a white background, but the heading above
is white on a navy background.
</body>
</html>
```

By changing the values in the style properties, you change the results you see in the browser. Look a Figure 10.2 to see how the following changes affect what you see. By not adding a separate font-color and background property to the <h1> tag, the properties assigned in the <body> tag continue.

```
<style type="text/css">
body {font-family:Trebuchet MS;
      color:black;
      font-size:12;
      background:FFFF80}
h1    {font-family:Bookman Old Style;
      font-size:14}
</style>
```

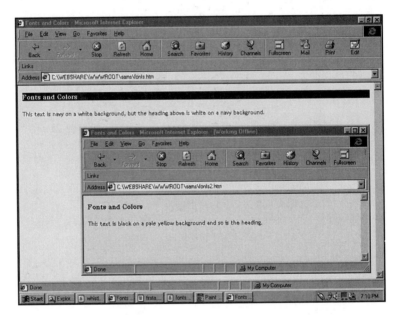

FIGURE 10.2 The background property sets the background color of the entire tag, so using the property on the <body> tag sets the color for the entire page.

> **Tip** Don't get carried away with your font selections. A good rule of thumb is to use no more than three different fonts on each page: one font for the headings, one for the body text, and one for any special text, such as captions and pull-quotes.

Images

Like the other design elements discussed in this chapter, you should use images sparingly when they support the theme you've already established. In Chapter 7, you learned how to add images to your Web pages and use HTML and style sheet properties to align them with your text. Figure 10.3 shows the difference balance and diversity make to your overall Web page layout.

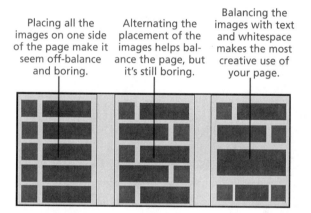

Placing all the images on one side of the page make it seem off-balance and boring.

Alternating the placement of the images helps balance the page, but it's still boring.

Balancing the images with text and whitespace makes the most creative use of your page.

FIGURE 10.3   Adding diversity to your graphical layout helps add interest.

Caution   Whenever you are working with graphics on a Web page, you need to be mindful of the overall size of the file. Most people will visit your Web site using a slow modem connection and might not be willing to wait for your page to finish loading. When you open your page using a 28.8kbs modem, it should take no longer than five seconds to load. If your pages take much longer to load, you might try to reduce the image size, add thumbnails, or include some type of warning as to the fact that the page will take longer to load.

Background Images

Earlier, you learned how to add a background color to your pages, but
sometimes you'll want to add an image to the background of your page.
The most prolific example of a background image is the page border (see
Figure 10.4).

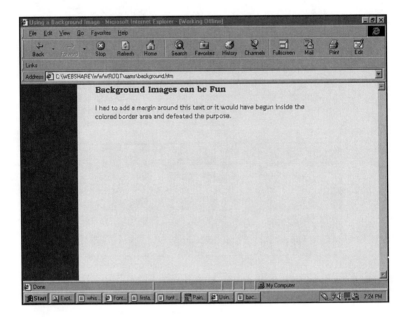

FIGURE 10.4   Use the background-image and margin style sheet
properties to create a colored border on your Web page.

Here's how the source code looks for that page.

```html
<html>
<head><title>Using a Background Image</title></head>
<style type="text/css">
body {font-family:Trebuchet MS, Arial;
        color:black;
        font-size:14;
        background-image:url(images\background.gif);
```

```
        background-position:left top;
        margin:0,160}
h1      {font-family:Bookman Old Style, Times New Roman;
        color:A00068;
        font-size:18;
        background:white}
</style>
<body>
<h1>Background Images can be Fun</H1>
I had to add a margin around this text or it would have begun
inside
the colored border area and defeated the purpose.
</body>
</html>
```

The background.gif image is the colored border background. It is a GIF
file, which makes it small (only 5k) so that it will load quickly. I made it
in Paint Shop Pro by drawing a rectangle down the side of the page, as
shown in Figure 10.5.

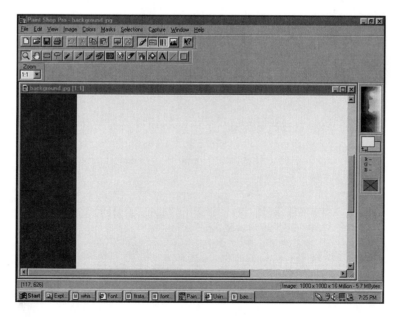

FIGURE 10.5   The background.gif file was created in Paint Shop
Pro.

You've already seen how you can use style sheet properties to set the fonts and colors of the page, but look at the HTML source code for Figure 10.4 again to see that we've added three new style sheet properties for you to learn:

- *Background-image:url*(url *of file)*—The property tells the browser where to find the background image you want to use on your page. It must be used as part of the body style.

- *Background-position*—This property tells the browser where to place the background image. This is assumed to be the top left (or left top), but you can specify any combination of the following vertical values: top, bottom, or center, and these horizontal values: left, right, or center.

- *Margin*—You can specify the margin property in inches (in), centimeters (cm), ems (em), points (pt), or pixels (px). If no unit of measure is specified, then the pixel unit is assumed. You can set the top, right, bottom, and left margins. I only set two of the margins for my background (0, 160). The browser knows that I wanted top=0px, right=160px, bottom=0px, and left=160px. The browser copied the first two values and applied the same values to the last two options. If I had only entered one value, the browser would have applied the same value to all four options.

If I hadn't set the margin property, the text on my page would have overlapped my image, as shown in Figure 10.6. The browser's even smart enough to add a white background to the heading text that overlaps the border.

 Tip Don't forget to check out Chapter 11 if you want to know more about HTML style sheets.

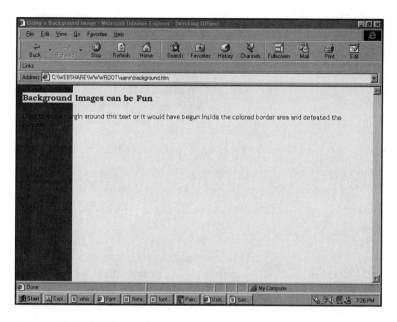

FIGURE 10.6 Without the margin property, text starts at the left edge of the page.

In this lesson, you've learned:

- The layout, images, navigation buttons, bullets, lines, colors, and even the fonts you choose should support the overall design theme of your site.

- Create interest in your Web pages by alternating the alignment of text and images, and by adding bulleted lists and tables.

- Just because you can specify a font doesn't mean that your visitor will have that font on his or her computer. To be on the safe side, always use Arial or Times New Roman as your alternate font.

LESSON 11
Adding Your Own Style

In this lesson, you'll learn how to create style sheets, apply them to your HTML pages, and wow your audience with your creativity.

Style Sheets

As you've already read, HTML was written as a markup language for defining the structure of a document (paragraphs, headings, tables, and so on). Although it was never intended to become a desktop publishing tool, it does include some basic formatting attributes, such as `bgcolor`, `font-size`, and `align`. In 1996, the W3C first recommended the idea of Cascading Style Sheets (CSS) to format HTML documents. The recommendation, which was updated in mid-1998, enables Web developers to separate the structure and format of their documents.

 Style sheet Set of *rules* that determine how the styles will be applied to the HTML tags in your documents.

The CSS recommendation describes the following three types of style sheets: embedded, inline, and linked.

- *Embedded*—The style properties are included (within the `<style>` tags) at the top of the HTML document. A style assigned to a particular tag will apply to all those tags in this document. So far in this book, you've seen examples of embedded style sheets.

- *Inline*—The style properties are included throughout the HTML page. Each HTML tag receives its own style attributes as they occur in the page.

- *Linked*—The style properties are stored in a separate file. That file can be linked to any HTML document with a `<link>` tag placed within the `<head>` tags.

In the following sections, you'll learn how to construct these style sheets and how to apply them to your documents.

Defining the Rules

Style sheet rules are made up of *selectors* (the HTML tags that will receive the style) and *declarations* (the style sheet properties and their values). In the following example, the selector is the body tag and the declaration is made up of the style property (background) and its value (black). This example would set the background color for the entire document to black.

```
body {background:black}
```

You can see that, in a style sheet, the HTML tag is not surrounded by brackets as it would be in the HTML document, and that the declaration is surrounded by curly braces. Declarations can contain more than one property. The following example also will set the text color for this page to white. Notice that the two properties are separated by a semicolon.

```
body {background:black; color:white}
```

You can format this style rule in a number of ways to make it easier to read. The following rule, for example, will produce exactly the same results as the preceding style.

```
body {background:black;
      color:white}
```

So will this.

```
body {
      background:black;
      color:white
      }
```

If you want to apply the same rules to several HTML tags, you could group those rules together, as in the following example.

```
body, td, h1 {
                background:black;
                color:white
                }
```

Add a Little `class`

As the old saying goes, rules are made to be broken. What if you don't want every single h1 heading in your document to be white on a black background? Maybe you want every other h1 heading to be yellow on a white background. Let me introduce you to the class attribute. You can apply this attribute to almost every HTML tag and it's almost like creating your own tags.

Figure 11.1 shows a fairly standard HTML page that uses an aqua table at the top of the page to hold the navigation links and places other tabular content in yellow tables throughout the document. You can see the HTML document for that page in Figure 11.2.

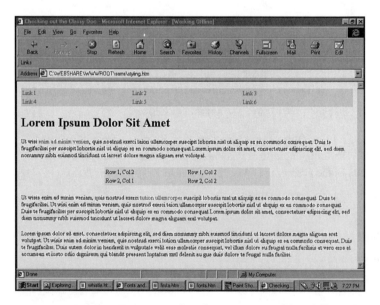

FIGURE 11.1 An HTML page that formats two tables differently.

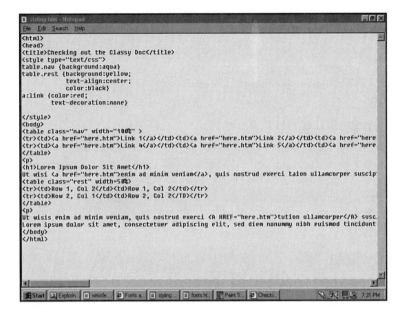

FIGURE 11.2 The HTML document for the page in Figure 11.1. Notice the class attribute in each <table> tag.

Take a closer look at the style properties in Figure 11.2. This document defines two table styles within the <style> tags. The HTML tag name table is followed by a period (.) and the class name ("nav" and "rest").

```
table.nav {background:aqua}
table.rest {background:yellow;
            text-align:center;
            color:black}
```

When the table is referenced in the body of the document, you must apply the class attribute to tell the browser which style properties should be applied. The HTML markup for each table in this example appears in the following HTML code. You can see that the class name appears within quotations just like the other HTML attributes (as with the width attribute shown here).

```
<table class="nav" width="100%">

<table class="rest" width=50%>
```

Applying Styles

Before moving on, we'll quickly cover how to apply style properties to your documents. Remember, three ways are available to add style sheets: embedded, linked, and inline. We'll discuss each one in turn.

Embedded Styles

All the styles are defined at the top of the HTML document within the <head> tags. The styles defined here will apply to only the one document in which they appear. If you plan to use these same styles in another document, you will need to add them there as well.

```
<head>
<style type="text/css">
table.nav {background:aqua}
table.rest {background:yellow;
            text-align:center;
            color:black}
a:link {color:red;
        text-decoration:none}
</style>
</head>
```

The <style> tag will almost always include the type="text/css" attribute, so you might as well get used to adding it.

Linked Styles

Linked style sheets hold all the style properties in a separate file. You then link the file into each HTML document where you want those style properties to appear.

```
<head>
<link rel="stylesheet" href="mystyles.css" type="text/css">
</head>
```

With this method, I've created a separate file called mystyles.css (for cascading style sheet) that contains all my style properties. You can see that the same type="text/css" attribute shows up here. Following are the entire contents of mystyles.css. These are the same styles that showed up in the preceding embedded styles example, but now they appear in a separate text file.

```
table.nav {background:aqua}
table.rest {background:yellow;
           text-align:center;
           color:black}
a:link {color:red;
        text-decoration:none}
```

> **Tip** In Chapter 10, "Designing with HTML," you
> learned that an effective, well-designed Web site
> (with more than one page) will contain repeated page
> elements and styles. The linked style sheet is most
> appropriate for this type of Web authoring.

Inline Styles

With inline styles, the style properties are added to the HTML tag as the
tag is entered. This means that if I want the same style to appear on all the
<h1> tags in my document, I would have to type those styles in all the
<h1> tags. Look at the following example. I am still using the same style
properties as in the previous examples, but now you can see how the two
tables would be created using inline styles.

```
<table style="background:aqua" width="100%">
```

```
<table style="background:yellow; text-align:center;
color:black" width="100%">
```

Using inline styles, the <style> tag becomes the style attribute. Multiple
style properties are still separated by semicolons, but the entire group of
properties for each tag are grouped within each HTML tag. This type of
style sheet is fine for documents in which you only need to apply style to
one or two elements, but you wouldn't want to have to go to all that work
when you have a lot of styles to add.

Cascading Precedence

You've got one more thing to learn before moving on. These three styles
are not treated equally by the browsers, nor are they supposed to be.

Web browsers will give precedence to the style that appears closest to the tag. So, inline styles (which appear as attributes within the tag itself) are most important; embedded styles (which appear at the top of the HTML file) will be applied next, and linked styles (which appear in another file altogether) will be applied next.

Imagine that you have created an embedded style for the <h1> tag, but want to change that style for one occurrence of the <h1> tag in that document. You would create an inline style for that new <h1> tag. The browsers recognize that fact and change the style for that tag to reflect the inline style.

> **Caution**   Style sheet precedence is supposed to place more importance on embedded styles than on linked style sheets, but in actual practice, you'll find that both Internet Explorer and Netscape actually treat linked sheets as more important than embedded sheets, although they do treat inline styles as more important than either of the other two. You'll find that you have better luck if you use either linked or embedded styles, but not both.

Style Sheet Properties

Now that you know how to format styles within a document, let's look at some of the different style properties you can apply.

Link Styles

You have seen those bright blue underlined hyperlinks on the Web. Style sheets have the following different selectors to help you change the look of them:

- a:link   Sets the styles for unvisited links.

- a:visited   Sets the styles for visited links.

- `a:active` Sets the styles for the hyperlink while it is linking.

- `a:hover` Sets the style for the link while your mouse is hovering.

> **Caution** None of the most popular Web browsers react the same to all the style sheet properties. Your best bet is to remember to test everything before you publish it. Web Review maintains a table of style sheet properties mapped to the most popular browsers. Check out this table (`http://webreview.com/wr/pub/guides/style/mastergrid.html`) to find out whether the style sheet properties you plan to use are supported by browsers.

Table 11.1 shows you some of the style properties you can assign to your links.

TABLE 11.1 Style Properties for the Anchor Styles

Property	Description of Use and Values
`background-color`	Sets the background color for the link.
`color`	Sets the text color for the link.
`font-family`	Sets the font for the text of the link.
`text-decoration`	Underline, overline, strikethrough, and none.

Font Styles

Text is the most important element of any Web page. Without text, there is no context to the page to help people decide whether it's worth it to come back.

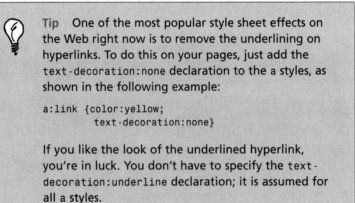

<del>Tip</del>

Tip   One of the most popular style sheet effects on the Web right now is to remove the underlining on hyperlinks. To do this on your pages, just add the `text-decoration:none` declaration to the a styles, as shown in the following example:

```
a:link {color:yellow;
        text-decoration:none}
```

If you like the look of the underlined hyperlink, you're in luck. You don't have to specify the `text-decoration:underline` declaration; it is assumed for all a styles.

Text on an HTML page is represented by the `<body>`, `<p>`, `<td>`, `<tr>`, `<th>`, `<h1>` through `<h6>`, and `<li>` tags, as well as others. You can add your own style preferences to each of these tags using the style properties shown in Table 11.2.

TABLE 11.2   Style Properties for Text

Property	Description of Use and Values
`background`	Sets the background color for the text.
`color`	Sets the text color for the text.
`font-family`	Sets the font for the text.
`font-size`	Can be a point size, a percentage of the size of another tag, or `xx-small` to `xx-large`.
`font-style`	`normal` (which is assumed) or `italic`.
`font-weight`	`extra-light` to `extra-bold`.
`text-align`	`left`, `right`, `center`, or `justify` (full).
`text-indent`	Can be a fixed length or a percentage.
`text-decoration`	`underline`, `overline`, `strikethrough`, and `none`.

Microsoft maintains several sample documents in their CSS Gallery
(`http://www.microsoft.com/typography/css/gallery/entrance.htm`)
to show Web page authors how style sheets can enhance their documents.
The <style> tag for one of those examples is shown in the following
code. This is impressive because of the many different styles and classes
defined in this document. You can see that you are only limited by your
own imagination. Be sure to see this style sheet in action on Microsoft's
Web site at `http://www.microsoft.com/truetype/css/`
`gallery/slide3.htm`.

```
<style type="text/css">
body {background: coral}
.copy {color: Black;
    font-size: 11px;
    line-height: 14px;
    font-family: Verdana, Arial, Helvetica, sans-serif }
a:link {text-decoration: none;
    font-size: 20px;
    color: black;
    font-family: Comic Sans MS, Arial Black, Arial, helvetica,
                 sans-serif}
.star {color: white;
    font-size: 350px;
    font-family: Arial, Arial, helvetica, sans-serif}
.subhead {color: black;
    font-size: 28px;
    margin-top: 12px;
    margin-left: 20px;
    line-height: 32px;
    font-family: Impact, Arial Black, Arial, helvetica,
                 sans-serif}
.what {color: black;
    font-size: 22px;
    margin-left: 20px;
    font-weight: bold;
    font-style: italic;
    font-family: Times New Roman, times, serif}
.quott {color: black;
    font-size: 120px;
    line-height: 120px;
    margin-top: -24px;
    margin-left: -4px;
    font-family: Arial Black, Arial, helvetica, sans-serif}
.quotb {color: black;
```

```
        font-size: 120px;
        line-height: 120px;
        margin-right: -1px;
        margin-top: -33px;
        font-family: Arial Black, Arial, helvetica, sans-serif}
.quote {color: red;
        font-size: 24px;
        line-height: 28px;
        margin-top: -153px;
        font-family: Impact, Arial Black, Arial, helvetica,
                     sans-serif}
.footer {color: cornsilk;
        background: red;
        font-size: 22px;
        margin-left: 20px;
        margin-top: 16px;
        font-family: Impact, Arial Black, Arial, helvetica,
                     sans-serif}
.headline {color: black;
        font-size: 80px;
        line-height: 90px;
        margin-left: 20px;
        font-family: Impact, Arial Black, Arial, helvetica,
                     sans-serif}
.mast {color: cornsilk;
        font-size: 90px;
        font-style: italic;
        font-family: Impact, Arial Black, Arial, helvetica,
                     sans-serif}
</style>
```

Color Styles

Chapter 10 discussed colors, but there are a few more things you can do with colors other than what was covered in that chapter. As you can see in Table 11.3, you can apply color to your HTML tags in two different ways: with color or background.

Tip   Check out http://wdvl.internet.com/
Authoring/Graphics/Colour/ for a quick tune-up of
Web color selections.

TABLE 11.3   Style Properties for Color

Property	Description of Use and Values
color	Sets the color of the text.
background	Sets the background of the page or text.

Caution   Don't forget to test your pages before you
publish them. Not all colors work together. If you've
specified a black background color and a black text
color, you've got a problem; no one will be able ,to
see your text.

Margin Styles

Style sheets give you another important advantage: you can specify the
margins of almost any HTML. The margins can be defined in pt, in, cm,
or px sizes.

```
body {margin-left:     100px;
      margin-right:    100px;
      margin-top:     50px}
```

You can set the margin-left, margin-right, and margin-top properties
individually, or combine them into one property called margin that applies
the sizes to the top, right, and then left margins.

```
body {margin: 100px 100px 50px}
```

The sample CSS document from Microsoft's CSS Gallery that you looked at
earlier also specifies margins for the text elements. Try it on your documents.

```
<style type="text/css">
body {background: coral }
```

```
.subhead { color: black;
    font-size: 28px;
    margin-top: 12px;
    margin-left: 20px;
    line-height: 32px;
    font-family: Impact, Arial Black, Arial, helvetica,
                 sans-serif}
</style>
```

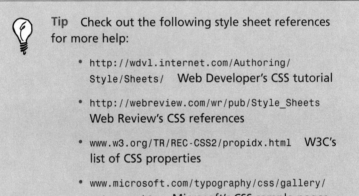

Tip Check out the following style sheet references for more help:

- http://wdvl.internet.com/Authoring/ Style/Sheets/ Web Developer's CSS tutorial

- http://webreview.com/wr/pub/Style_Sheets Web Review's CSS references

- www.w3.org/TR/REC-CSS2/propidx.html W3C's list of CSS properties

- www.microsoft.com/typography/css/gallery/ entrance.htm Microsoft's CSS sample pages

Table 11.4 lists the HTML tags that were discussed in this lesson.

TABLE 11.4   HTML Tags Used in This Lesson

HTML Tag	Closing	Description of Use
<style>	</style>	Surrounds style sheet properties, or references to external style sheets.

In this lesson, you've learned:

- The CSS recommendation describes three types of style sheets: embedded, inline, and linked.

- If multiple style sheets are applied to your HTML document, the browser will apply the styles of the inline style sheet first, then the linked style sheets, then embedded style sheets.

- Remove the underlining on your hyperlinks by adding the `text-decoration:none` declaration to your a styles tags.

LESSON 12
Creating Frames

In this lesson, you'll learn to create frames. You'll also learn why some people don't like them and how you can use them effectively.

Simple Frames

HTML *frames* give you a way to display two or more HTML documents at once. Each frame in the browser window displays its own HTML document. Those documents can link to each other or remain completely separate entities.

 Frame A complete HTML document that appears inside of, or alongside, one or more other HTML documents within the same browser window.

Most often, as in Figure 12.1, you'll see frames used as a navigation bar on a Web site. The navigation frame can appear on any edge of the document, but you'll probably find it on the top or left margins, since English (the language of most Web pages) is oriented from top to bottom and left to right.

Frame border

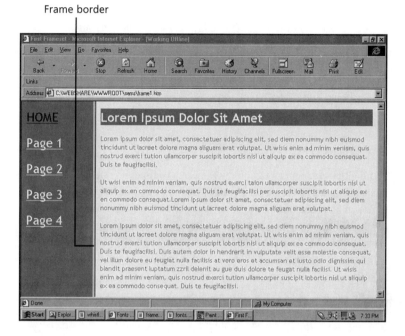

FIGURE 12.1 A simple two-frame document as it appears in the browser. The left frame contains the site's navigation bar and the right frame contains the pages to which the navigation buttons link.

To create frames, you'll need to create a new type of HTML document, called a frameset. A *frameset* is a special type of HTML document that defines how many frames will be displayed and which HTML documents will appear in each frame. The frameset document for the page is displayed in Figure 12.1.

```
<html>
<head><title>First Frameset</title></head>
<style type=text/css>
</style>
<frameset cols="20%,*">
<frame src="toc.htm" name="left">
<frame src="latin.htm" name="main">
<noframes><a href="toc.htm">Table of Contents</a></noframes>
</frameset>
</html>
```

If you compare this document with a regular HTML document, you should notice right away that the <body> tag is missing. A frameset document uses a new tag, <frameset>, to replace the <body> tag. Within the <frameset> tag, you'll see the <frame> tag, which is used to describe the contents of each frame, and the <noframes> tag, which is used to instruct the browser what to display in the event the viewer's browser does not support frames. Let's take a closer look at each of these tags.

\<frameset\>

Within the <frameset> tag, you will need to define the orientation of the frames—in vertical columns, cols, or in horizontal rows, rows. This orientation attribute also requires that you define the size of each of your frames. If you have three vertical frames in your frameset, for example, you will need to specify three size attributes. Look again at the <frameset> tag in the preceding HTML sample.

```
<frameset cols="20%,*">
```

This tag defines two vertical columns. The first column is 20 percent of the screen width, the second column fills the remainder of the screen—80 percent. The asterisk (*) tells the browser to fill the remainder of the screen. You can use the same trick if you are defining more than two frames. Although it shows only two values, the following <frameset> tag will actually be used to define *three* horizontal rows. The first row has been set to 20 percent of the length of the screen; the asterisk forces the browser to equally divide the remainder of the screen between the other two rows.

```
<frameset rows="20%,*">
```

You don't have to let the browser figure out the size of your frames. If you are a perfectionist, you can do your own math and specify the size yourself. Just remember that the total value of the sizes can't be more than 100 percent of the screen. Now that makes sense, doesn't it?

>
>
> **Tip**   You can specify the size of your frames in pixels or as a percentage of the browser window by using the % sign as in the following tag:
>
> `<frameset cols="50%,50%">`.
>
> You don't have to use the % sign, however. You can use a forward slash (/) as an abbreviation of the % sign, as in the following tag:
>
> `<frameset cols="50/,50/">`.

`<frame>`

Like the `<img>` tag you learned about in Chapter 7, "Adding Images," the `<frame>` tag uses the src (source) attribute to tell the browser where to find the document to display. The important thing to remember when you are setting up your frameset document is that you are defining the start page for your Web site—or the first framed page in your site. You don't have to figure out every possible combination of pages that might appear—you only have to specify the first one.

The `<frame>` tag also requires a name attribute. Most people name their frames by their location on the browser window. The `<frame>` tags in the preceding example, for instance, call the frame that appears on the left of the screen, left, and the other frame main because it will hold the main pages of the Web site.

```
<frame src="toc.htm" name="left">
<frame src="latin.htm" name="main">
```

> **Tip**   You could name the frames anything (Dog, Cat, Red, or Blue), but you'll find them easier to remember if you stick to the basics.

Following are a few more attributes of the <frame> tag that might come in handy:

- frameborder   With this attribute, you can remove the small border line that separates borders. In Figure 12.2, the border has been removed from the sample frameset.

- marginwidth or marginheight   These attributes specify (in pixels) the space between the border and the text in the frame.

- scrolling   Using the values of yes, no, or auto, you can tell the browser whether or not to add a scrollbar next to the frame. Don't worry, however; even if you've specified scrolling="no", the browser will display a scrollbar if the content of the frame exceeds the size of the frame.

- noresize   Just like any other window, you can resize frames manually by dragging the frame's border (even when the frameborder="0" attribute has been specified). You can avoid that by specifying the noresize attribute in your frameset.

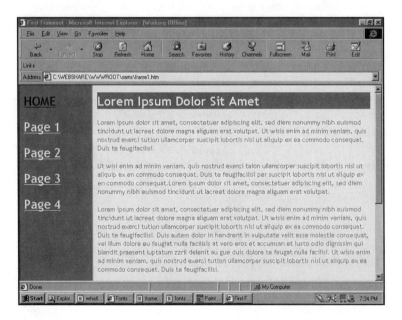

FIGURE 12.2   Figure 12.1 with the frameborder attribute set to "0".

<noframes>

The <noframes> tag that appears in the preceding example tells the browser what to do if it doesn't know how to display frames, or if your visitor has adjusted his browser's settings to refuse frames.

```
<noframes><a href="toc.htm">Table of Contents</a></noframes>
```

The <noframes> tag is not required and many Web page authors choose to ignore it, but it takes very little effort to add it and it makes good sense if you want to be certain that everyone will be able to view your Web site.

While it's true that many authors ignore the <noframes> tag, you'll find that just as many authors choose to create an entire non-framed version of their Web site. I happen to think that's overkill. Particularly, if you are using frames as a navigation bar, you could make a couple simple changes to your main HTML pages to help people who can't see the frames navigate through your site. In Figure 12.3, I've made the frameset from Figure 12.1 into a non-framed version by adding a simple one-row table to hold the navigation elements.

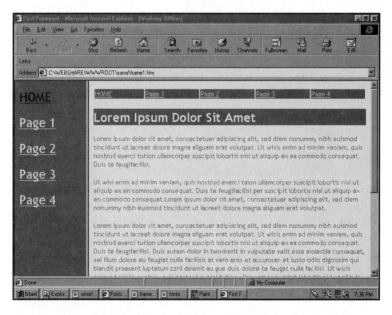

FIGURE 12.3 Adding a navigation bar to the top of each of the main pages will make this site work for those people who can't view framed pages.

Nested Frames

You might want to be more creative with your frame layout. You can use the `<frameset>` tag more than once in a single frameset document. This feature enables you to nest frames within each other. Following is an example of a nested frame. I indented the second `<frameset>` to make it easier to read.

```
<html>
<head><title>First Frameset</title></head>
<style type=text/css>
</style>
<frameset rows="15%,*,10%">
<frame src="sitename.htm" name="top">
  <frameset cols="20%,*,11%">
  <frame src="toc.htm" name="left">
  <frame src="latin.htm" name="main">
  <frame src="motto.htm" name="right">
  </frameset>
<frame src="contacts.htm" name="bottom">
<noframes><a href="toc.htm">Table of Contents</a></noframes>
</frameset>
</html>
```

The first `<frameset>` tag defines three horizontal frames, but the second `<frameset>` tag divides the middle row into three column frames. Figure 12.4 shows you how this nested frameset will appear in the browser.

`<iframe>`

You can create a frame another way by using the `<iframe>`, or inline frame, tag. Rather than creating a separate frameset document, you define an inline frame within a regular HTML document because it appears in the middle of another document. Figure 12.5 shows the same content as the sample in Figure 12.4, but this page was created using an inline frame. You can see the HTML document for this page in Figure 12.6.

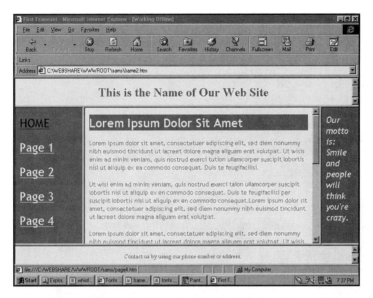

FIGURE 12.4 All the borders have been left showing to help you see where the nested frames are in this example.

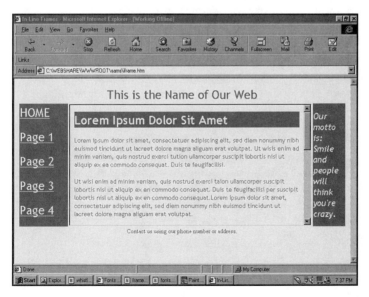

FIGURE 12.5 The scrollable document in the center of this page was added with an inline frame.

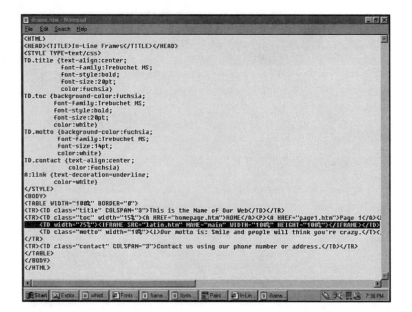

FIGURE 12.6   Style sheet properties are used to help define the colors and fonts for this document. The `<iframe>` tag actually is embedded inside a table to achieve the page layout shown in Figure 12.5.

You can apply all the same attributes for regular frames to the `<iframe>` tag except the `noresize` attribute, because unlike regular frames, inline frames cannot be resized.

> **Caution**   As of right now, the `<iframe>` tag only works with Internet Explorer 4 and higher browsers, so don't try to use it unless you know your audience has that browser.

> Tip   Throughout the book, you have been cautioned
> that not all browsers support all the HTML tags you've
> learned. StatMarket tracks browser usage and other
> fun statistics on their Web site
> (www.statmarket.com/SM?c=Browsers). You can use
> that knowledge to decide whether you are willing to
> take the risk of using a tag such as <iframe>, which is
> not supported by all browsers.

Linking Between Frames

Think back to Chapter 5, "Linking Text and Documents," when you
learned how to create hyperlinks. You'll remember that you can use the <a
name="*named anchor*"> tag to name an anchor, or target, within a document that could be linked to directly, as shown in the following code.

```
<a name="PointA">Point A</a>
```

You'll remember that you need to use the anchor tag, <a
href="*url#anchor*">, to surround the text that you want to highlight, as
shown in the following example:

```
<a href="DOC2.htm#PointA">Click Here to go to Point A</a>
```

All frames have a name attribute assigned to them. You can use that name
to specify which frame you want your hyperlink to open in. Let's look at
the HTML code for the toc.htm file used in the preceding examples.

```
<html>
<head><title>Table of Contents</title></head>
<style type=text/css>
</style>
<body>
<a href="homepage.htm" target="main">HOME</a><p>
<a href="page1.htm" target="main">Page 1</a><p>
<a href="page2.htm" target="main">Page 2</a><p>
<a href="page3.htm" target="main">Page 3</a><p>
<a href="page4.htm" target="main">Page 4</a><p>
</body>
</html>
```

Now you see a new attribute has been attached to the `<a href>` tag: target. The `target` attribute refers to the *target frame* for the hyperlink. Besides the frame names that you've specified in your frameset document, you can target the following other three names:

- `<a href="url" target="blank">`   This tag opens the hyperlink in a new browser window.

- `<a href="url" target="self">`   This tag opens the hyperlink in the same window where the hyperlink was. If the hyperlink was in a frame, the link will open in the same frame, replacing that frame document.

- `<a href="url" target="top">`   This tag opens the hyperlink in the same browser window. If the hyperlink was in a frame, the link will open in the same frame, replacing thefollowing entire frameset.

Target frame   The name of the frame in which a hyperlink will open.

Caution   Always specify the target attribute whenever you are working with frames. If you don't specify the target frame, the browser generally will replace the current frame with the target document, which probably is not what you'd intended.

The Two Biggest Problems with Frames

Mention frames to any Web site developer and you'll be sure to get an earful—good or bad; people always have an opinion. You've already seen how useful they can be at providing navigation information, but let's see why so many people dislike them.

> **Tip** Jakob Nielsen, undoubtedly the Web's most respected Usability expert, maintains a Web page called (and pardon my French), Why Frames Suck (Most of the Time), in which he discusses some of the many problems users have with frames. You can read his article at www.useit.com/alertbox/9612.html.

So Many Pages, So Few URLs

When you load your frameset document into your browser, you are telling the browser to load all the pages into this same document, following the selected hyperlinks. So? Take a look at the URL for your frameset document. My URL is C:\Webshare\wwwroot\sams\frame2.htm. No matter how many times I click on the hyperlinks in my framed pages, the URL stays the same because all those framed pages are loading into the same frameset document.

Why is that a problem? Suppose that my best customer is browsing my site and she is looking at the *wonderful* information on Page4.htm. She decides to save the URL so that she doesn't have to look for the information again. The URL she saves is C:\Webshare\wwwroot\sams\frame2.htm, not C:\Webshare\wwwroot\sams\page4.htm, which is what she was actually looking at. There is no guarantee that when she opens that URL in the browser, it will open on Page4.htm, as she wanted in the first place. How frustrating!

If you right-click the mouse (or hold the mouse button if you have a Macintosh), you can click on Properties in the shortcut menu. On the Properties dialog box is the URL for that particular page (see Figure 12.7). You can highlight and copy that URL into the Address field of your browser to open later. When you do this, however, you will not see the framed version of the site; you will only see the single document that you saved, with no additional navigation to help you.

![Properties dialog box screenshot]

Properties	
General	

Definition Lists

Protocol: File Protocol

Type: Internet Document (HTML)

Address: file:///C:/WEBSHARE/WWWROOT/.../ann/latin.htm
(URL)

Undo
Cut
Copy
Paste
Delete

Size: 2726 bytes

Select All

Created: Wednesday, J...
Modified: Wednesday, July 14, 1999

Certificates | Analyze

OK | Cancel

FIGURE 12.7   The Properties dialog box contains the actual URL for a framed page. You can copy the URL using the shortcut menu after you highlight the text.

Printing

Another huge problem for users of your framed Web site is *printing*. Why should printing be a problem? As much as we like to think that we are headed toward paperless offices and online commerce, people still like to print documents. When most people see a page that they want to print, they click the Print button on their browser. With frames, the Print button only prints the *active frame*.

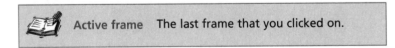

Active frame   The last frame that you clicked on.

On my sample framed site, if you clicked on a link in the left frame to open a new document in the main frame and then clicked the Print button without making any other mouse clicks, you would actually print the navigation bar on the left frame, not the document in the main frame that you wanted. Unfortunately, the browser doesn't know which frame you want, only which frame was last active.

The newer browser versions have included a new feature in their Print dialog boxes—a Print Frames option that allows you to specify whether you want to print the active frame or the entire frameset (see Figure 12.8). That's an improvement, but it requires extra clicks (and some know-how).

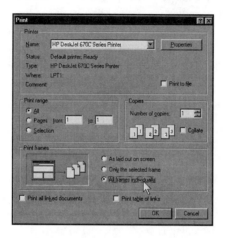

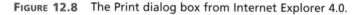

FIGURE 12.8   The Print dialog box from Internet Explorer 4.0.

> **Tip**   If you want to print a single frame, you can click the right-mouse button, or hold down the mouse button if you are using a Macintosh, and select the Print option from the shortcut menu. The printer will print only the selected frame, not the entire frameset.

Using Frames Effectively

Although frames have some usability problems, there are some obvious advantages for using them. Just make sure that you use them the right way. Here are some tips to help.

- *Frames are not a toy*—Frames work best when used as a navigation tool, or when it makes sense to show two or more elements of a document at the same time.

- *Remember the target attribute*—Nothing is worse than when you click on a hyperlink in a framed document and break out of frames unintentionally. Worse, each hyperlink in a framed document that does not include the target attribute has the potential of opening in a new browser window. You could end up with a real mess.

- *Include the <noframes> tag*—Always remember that there are people who can't see frames (either because of older browsers, or because they set their browser preferences to ignore them). Provide alternate content with the <noframes> tag.

- *Never frame other framed pages*—Not as frequent anymore on the Web, but when frames first became available, Web page authors framed everything, including other framesets. This compound-framing is very confusing to users.

TABLE 12.1   HTML Tags Used in This Lesson

HTML Tag	Closing	Description of Use
<a href>	</a>	Creates hyperlinks to other documents. Always use the target attribute with frames.
<frameset>	</frameset>	Replaces the <body> tag in a frameset document and surrounds the <frame> and <noframes> tags. This tag must include the attribute to describe the orientation of the frames and their size.

HTML Tag	Closing	Description of Use
`<frame>`		Includes the frame's name and a URL for the content (`src`). It also might include attributes to define the `border` and `scrolling`.
`<iframe>`		Embeds a frame inside another document. It only works with Internet Explorer.
`<noframes>`	`</noframes>`	Defines an alternate viewing page for browsers that don't support frames.

In this lesson, you've learned:

- A frameset document defines the number of frames and their sizes; standard HTML documents will be contained in the frames.

- Each frame of a frameset document must be named so that you can direct your hyperlink to appear in a specific *target* frame.

- Despite their obvious advantage for organizing your site's navigation elements, many people dislike the usability problems associated with frames.

LESSON 13

Creating Forms

In this lesson, you'll learn how to create Web forms that enable you to get input from your visitors.

Creating Forms

You've seen forms on the Web, but I'll bet you didn't know they were so easy to create. I want to point out a couple of things for you to keep track of as you read this section and then you'll create a form.

- Forms are made up of fields (that you want the user to fill out) and buttons (to perform actions such as submit and reset).

- Every field (`<input type="type">` should have a `name` attribute as well.

- Every field can be set to have a default value (a preselected option that the users can overwrite if they want); many also can be set to validate the data the user enters.

- Every form requires a `submit` button that sends the form data to the address specified in the `action` attribute of the `<form>` tag. It has its own `<input>` tag and you can read more about it in the "Buttons" section later in this lesson.

One more thing: a form isn't a form until it is enclosed within the `<form>` tags. The `<form>` tag always includes an `action` and a `method` attribute. To make it simple, a form's `method` is almost always set to *post* and the `action` can only be one of two values: an email address of the person who will be receiving the form's data, or a URL of a file that will be receiving the form's data. We're going to use the email option because it's easier for you to practice with. Following is a simple <form> tag, but Figure 13.2 shows the full HTML document, including the <form> tag, for the form shown in Figure 13.1.

```
<form action="post" method="mailto:youremail@yourisp.com">
```

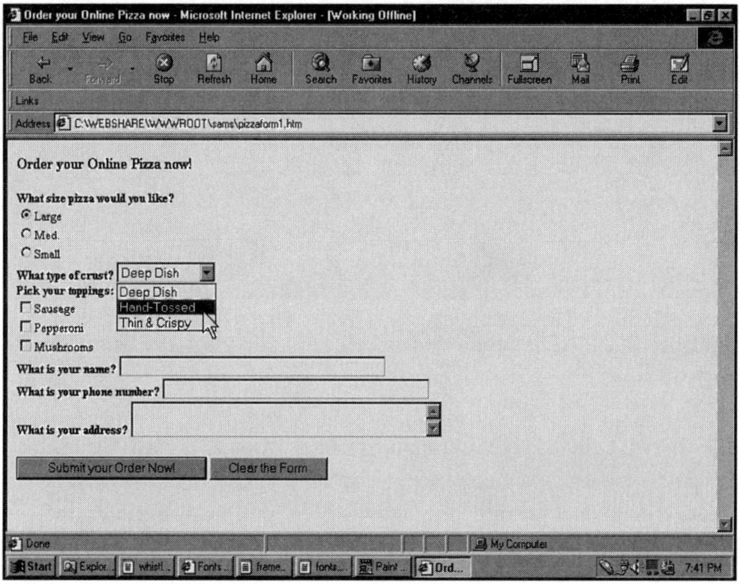

FIGURE 13.1   This Web form contains each of the input types (fields) available.

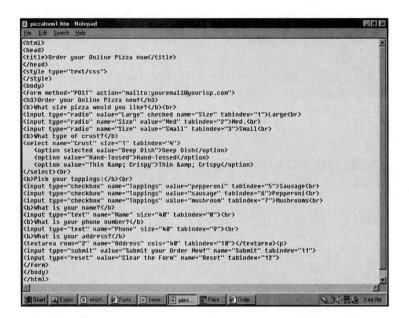

```
pizzaform1.htm - Notepad
File  Edit  Search  Help
<html>
<head>
<title>Order your Online Pizza now</title>
</head>
<style type="text/css">
</style>
<body>
<form method="POST" action="mailto:youremail@yourisp.com">
<h3>Order your Online Pizza now!</h3>
<b>What size pizza would you like?</b><br>
<input type="radio" value="Large" checked name="Size" tabindex="1">Large<br>
<input type="radio" name="Size" value="Med" tabindex="2">Med.<br>
<input type="radio" name="Size" value="Small" tabindex="3">Small<br>
<b>What type of crust?</b>
<select name="Crust" size="1" tabindex="4">
   <option selected value="Deep Dish">Deep Dish</option>
   <option value="Hand-Tossed">Hand-Tossed</option>
   <option value="Thin &amp; Crispy">Thin &amp; Crispy</option>
</select><br>
<b>Pick your toppings:</b><br>
<input type="checkbox" name="Toppings" value="pepperoni" tabindex="5">Sausage<br>
<input type="checkbox" name="Toppings" value="sausage" tabindex="6">Pepperoni<br>
<input type="checkbox" name="Toppings" value="mushroom" tabindex="7">Mushrooms<br>
<b>What is your name?</b>
<input type="text" name="Name" size="40" tabindex="8"><br>
<b>What is your phone number?</b>
<input type="text" name="Phone" size="40" tabindex="9"><br>
<b>What is your address?</b>
<textarea rows="2" name="Address" cols="40" tabindex="10"></textarea><p>
<input type="submit" value="Submit your Order Now!" name="Submit" tabindex="11">
<input type="reset" value="Clear the Form" name="Reset" tabindex="12">
</form>
</body>
</html>
```

FIGURE 13.2   Here's the HTML document for the form shown in Figure 13.1.

Don't forget that an HTML form is just like any other HTML document; it doesn't recognize extra spaces. If you want to line up your fields for a more professional looking form, line up your form fields in tables, as shown in Figure 13.3, and use style sheet properties to define your fonts and add images.

Form Fields

The only reason to create a form is to collect data. The fields on a form help you do that. The following sections describe each of the field types and give you some hints for how each one can be customized to suit your needs.

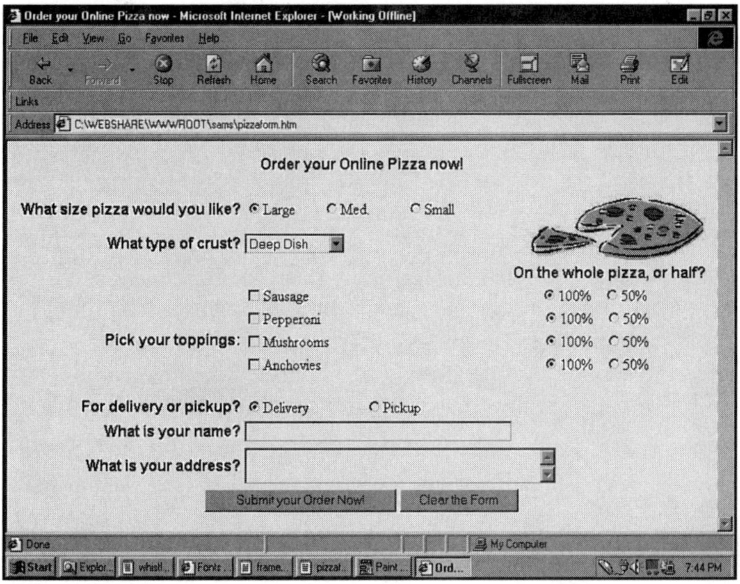

FIGURE 13.3 This version of the form took a little longer to create, but the results are worth it.

Text Box

The simplest form of data collection is an empty box. Your form poses a question ("What is your name?") and your visitor fills in the answer in the space provided. In HTML, this type of field is called a *text box*. HTML uses the <input> command to identify a form field. The following example is a complete HTML form with one field—a text box—that is 40 pixels wide and is called *Name*.

```
<form method="POST" action=mailto:youremail@yourisp.com>
<b>What is your name?</b>
<input type="text" name="Name" size="40"><br>
<input type="submit" value="Submit" name="submit">
</form>
```

The form field's attributes (type, name, and size) help to customize the form field. name and size are obvious, but the type attribute could use some explanation. Although this type of field traditionally is called a *text* box, you also can set the type attribute to *integer* (which is a whole number without decimals), *number* (which can include decimals), and *password* (which displays an asterisk (*) when the user types their password).

> **Tip** The tabindex attribute sets the order in which the user can navigate through the form elements using the Tab key. In Figure 13.2, you can see that each <input> tag includes a tabindex attribute and the index number increases toward the bottom of the form.

Text Area

You use the <textarea> tag to define a multi-line text box. In addition to the usual name and tabindex attributes, all <textarea> boxes should control the size of the box using the rows and cols attributes. cols indicates the width of the field in pixels; rows indicates the height of the field.

Anything you type between the <textarea> and </textarea> tags will appear inside the field and can be overwritten by users when they are completing the form. The following example shows the code for a text area box with an initial value of "Enter the address here."

```
<textarea name="address" rows="2" cols"80" tabindex="10">Enter
the address here.</textarea>
```

Radio Buttons and Check Boxes

Radio button and check box fields are very similar. In fact, there's really only one real difference between them: your user can select only one item in a radio button list, but can select multiple check box items. Look at the form in Figure 13.1 again. Check boxes are used for the pizza toppings question because it is possible that your visitors might want multiple toppings. Radio buttons are used to ask about the preferred size of the pizza because only one pizza at a time can be ordered with this form.

The following example demonstrates how a check box field is created. Notice that all the check box fields that relate to the same question ("Pick your toppings") have the same name attribute. You use the value attribute to specify the information you will see when the form data is submitted to you. If you don't specify any value, the form data typically will send on/off or yes/no values for all fields.

```
<input type="checkbox" name="toppings"
value="sausage">Sausage<br>
<input type="checkbox" name="toppings"
value="pepperoni">Pepperoni<br>
<input type="checkbox" name="toppings"
value="mushrooms">Mushrooms
```

With radio buttons, you'll need to use the checked attribute to set a starting value for each field. When you do specify a preselected option, be sure to select the most frequently submitted value. In the following example, the large pizza has been preselected. Users can change that selection when they are completing the form and the form data will be submitted to you with the users' choices selected.

```
<input type="radio" value="large" name="size"
checked>Large<br>
<input type="radio" value="med" name="size">Medium<br>
<input type="radio" value="small" name="size">Small<br>
```

Drop-down Option

The drop-down menu option, shown in the following HTML sample, uses a <select> tag to define the overall menu (such as giving it a name and a size—the number of rows visible at any time). Enclosed within the <select> tag are <option> tags that describe the contents of the drop-down menu. As with radio buttons, you can specify a start value for the drop-down menu using the selected attribute.

```
<select name="crust" size="1">
    <option value="Deep Dish" selected>Deep Dish</option>
    <option value="Hand-Tossed">Hand-Tossed</option>
    <option value="Thin &amp; Crispy">Thin &amp;
    Crispy</option>
</select>
```

> **Tip**   Some form designers like to add an <option> tag at the top of their drop-down menu fields that tells their users to select one of the items from the list. The drop-down menu field in Figure 13.4 demonstrates this option.

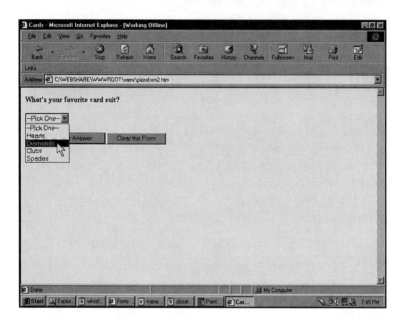

FIGURE 13.4   This drop-down menu includes an extra <option> tag for the Pick One statement.

Like check boxes, your user can select multiple options in the drop-down menu by adding the multiple attribute to the <select> tag. This change (shown in the following HTML sample) enables users to select multiple options by pressing and holding down the CTRL key while clicking on the options in the menu.

```
<FORM method="POST" action=mailto:youremail@yourisp.com >
<H3>What's your favorite card suit(s)?</H3>
<select name="suit" size="1" multiple>
```

```
       <option value="Hearts">Hearts</option>
       <option value="Diamonds">Diamonds</option>
       <option value="Clubs">Clubs</option>
       <option value="Spades">Spades</option>
</select>
```

Buttons

The Submit and Reset buttons are special types of form elements.
Although they are created using the <input> tag (see Figure 13.4), they
are not data collection tools, but actually are data *submission* tools.

- The Submit button collects all the data from the form and *posts*
  (sends) it to the location specified in the action portion of the
  <form> tag.

- The Reset button clears the form of any data that might have
  already been completed. The Reset button *resets* the form to the
  original preselected values.

The Submit button is required on all forms, but the Reset button is
optional. The browser's Refresh button has the same effect as the Reset
button on a form. It reloads the page and deletes everything except the initial values of the form.

Receiving Form Data

When your visitors click the Submit button on a form on your Web site,
the data they entered into the form will be sent to you using the action
you specified in your <form> tag. In Figure 13.2, we selected an email
action. Figure 13.5 shows you how my email software returns the form
data to me. You should now see why it is so important to include the name
attribute with every form field.

```
From: yourvisitor@hisisp.com
To: youremail@yourisp.com
Subject: Form

Size=Large
Crust=Deep Dish
Toppings=pepperoni+sausage
Name=your Visitor's Name
Phone=your Visitor's Phone number
Address=your Visitor's Address
```

FIGURE 13.5 Your email software may format the responses differently, but they will all show the field name (Size and Toppings, for example), along with the data your visitor entered into those fields.

It is not always convenient to receive form data via email, particularly if you expect to receive a lot of responses. Reading, and responding to, that many email messages can become tiresome. Your ISP also might prefer that you do not use its mail servers in this manner.

Another action that you can assign to your forms is a script to handle the responses for you. Scripts are automated form handlers and can be used to collect all the responses in a single file and respond to the visitors for you. This book can't begin to explain how to write the scripts, or find them, but your ISP, or your network administrator, probably will have several scripts available for you to choose from and can help you attach them to your form The important thing to remember is "Ask."

Table 13.1 lists the HTML tags that were discussed in this lesson.

TABLE 13.1 HTML Tags Used in This Lesson

HTML Tag	Closing	Description of Use
<form>	</form>	Encloses all form elements.
<input>		Identifies a form field.
<option>	</option>	Identifies the contents of a drop menu.
<select>	</select>	Encloses a drop-down menu field.
<textarea>	</textarea>	Identifies a multi-lined text field.

In this lesson, you've learned:

- All form fields should have a name and a tab order.

- The `<form>` tag always includes a `method` attribute (which is usually *post*) and an `action` attribute. The `action` can be either an email address or a URL of a file that will be receiving the form's data.

- The five form field types are: text box, text area, radio buttons, check boxes, and drop-down option menus.

LESSON 14
Creating Active Web Pages

In this lesson, you'll learn about some of the advanced scripting tools that can enhance your Web pages. You'll also find some resources to help you learn more.

What Are Active Web Pages?

Normal HTML pages—everything you've created so far—are considered to be *static*. The page you create is the page that your visitors will see and (assuming that the pages are created without browser-specific code) all your visitors will see the same thing.

Web applications and scripts allow your pages to change dynamically. You can use these techniques to make items onscreen change in relation to actions, such as a mouse click, that your visitors make.

Don't be scared off by the word *application*. There is some programming knowledge that will be required to implement these elements into your Web pages, but not much. Unfortunately, I can't teach you everything there is to know about programming, but I can tell you where to find additional information.

The most popular ways of including active elements in your Web pages are described in the sections that follow. Table 14.1 gives a quick overview of the information in this chapter.

TABLE 14.1 Scripting and Programming

Technique	Browser	Comments
ActiveX	Microsoft Explorer Internet	ActiveX will work on Netscape with a plug-in
DHTML	All	Microsoft and Netscape disagree on how to implement DHTML. You will likely end up creating two sets of code to make everyone happy.
Java	All	Platform independent and can be used to create complex applications.
JavaScript	All	The best of everything. Works on all browsers, can be called from a plain HTML page, and you can find plenty of examples to copy into your own Web pages.
VBScript	IE	Easier to learn, but works on Internet Explorer only.

Java and ActiveX

Java and ActiveX are used to create Web applications. Both Java (originated by Sun Microsystems) and ActiveX (created by Microsoft) are platform independent—meaning that PCs, Macintosh computers, and UNIX systems can interpret the commands in the application. ActiveX, however, only works with the Internet Explorer browser, which is nearly impossible to guarantee your users will use unless you use the annoying tactic so many developers have chosen—preceding any application with a note that warns your users that they will have to download the *right* browser before they can view your pages.

How Do They Work?

Both Java and ActiveX work under the principal of object-oriented programming. The idea is that each piece of code should be treated as a separate entity that can be used repeatedly in many types of environments, including the Web.

Both these elements can be embedded into your Web pages using HTML's <object> tag. An <object>, in HTML, can be an image, an application, or another HTML document. The attributes are the important distinction. The first example (that follows) would be used to include a Java application. The second example would be used to include an ActiveX control (application).

```
<object codetype="application/java-archive"
        codebase="http://www.myWeb.com/apps/"
        classid="java:my.program.start">
</object>

<object codebase="http://www.myWeb.com/apps/"
        data="my.activex.program">
        classid="CLSID:613C8CCE-1FF8-41CF-A3DB-052336C14002"
</object>
```

In the first example, the classid attribute is the name of the Java applet being called by the <object> tag. This same information appears in the data attribute for ActiveX programs. In both examples, the codebase attribute indicates the directory in which the application can be found. However, the codebase attribute itself is not necessary; the entire URL (including the base directory information) could be included in the classid (for Java) and data (for ActiveX) attributes rather than including the separate codebase attribute.

The ActiveX classid attribute deserves some explanation. Other than to tell you that the string of letters and numbers actually represents a URL, the best help I can give you is to tell you that any ActiveX control that you choose to include in your Web page will include the appropriate classid information so that you can copy it into your tag.

> **Tip**   Find information about Java and download some
> fun Java applets at
> www.javasoft.com/applets/index.html.
>
> You can find downloadable ActiveX controls at
> www.download.com/PC/Activex/. You can find a
> plug-in to run these controls on Netscape at
> www.ncompass.com/.

JavaScript and VBScript

Scripting is another type of programming, but it's easier to learn, which is
a plus. Scripts can be added to an HTML document using the `<script>`
tag. The tag *can* appear in the `<head>` or `<body>` of the document, but usually is added to the `<body>` tag.

A script may be contained in a separate document that is called by the
`<script>` tag (much as a linked style sheet is a separate document called by
the `<style>` tag. A script also may be contained within the `<script>` tags in
the HTML document itself. The decision is yours, based on how often you
plan to use the script. If the script will appear in only one page, then incor-
porate the script into the document, as in the first of the following HTML
samples. If the script will appear on more than one page, make it a separate
file so that you don't have to duplicate it, as in the second HTML sample.

```
<script type="text/vbscript">enter your script here.</script>
```

```
<script type="text/javascript"
src="http://www.myweb.com/scripts/myscript.jss"></script>
```

While the `src` (source) attribute is only required if the script is contained in
a separate file, the `type` attribute is always required. This attribute tells the
browser which language the script is written in: `text/javascript`,
`text/vbscript`, or `text/tcl`. If you are using the same scripting language
throughout your HTML document, you can include a `<meta>` tag that
defines the default script type for the entire document. The `<meta>` tag, as
you learned in Chapter 9, "Even More Tags," is placed inside the `<head>` tag
and gives the browser information about the document.

```
<meta http-equiv="Content-Script-Type" content="type">
```

What Can It Do?

The easy answer to this question is this: Anything. If you look at some of the script collections on the Web, you'll find that people are using script for anything, including adding table values, creating rollover effects, and even games.

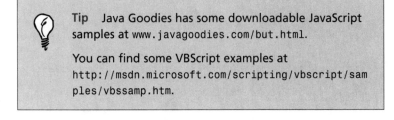

Tip   Java Goodies has some downloadable JavaScript samples at www.javagoodies.com/but.html.

You can find some VBScript examples at http://msdn.microsoft.com/scripting/vbscript/sam ples/vbssamp.htm.

It is possible to associate a script with a certain event that occurs when the page appears on the browser. Figure 14.1 is an HTML page with some very simple JavaScript code that changes the background color of the page with the press of a button.

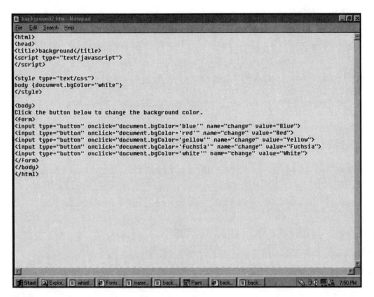

FIGURE 14.1   Simple JavaScript code to change the background color with the `onclick` command.

In looking at the code, you might wonder where the code is because the <script> tag is empty. The code in this case is embedded in the <input> tag with the onclick command. The tag will respond to each of the events shown in Table 14.2 and a few more.

TABLE 14.2 Script Calls

Event	With Tags	The script runs when...
onload	<body>, <frameset>	The document opens.
onunload	<body>, <frameset>	The document closes.
onclick	anything	The mouse is clicked over a particular item (button, image, and so on).
ondblclick	anything	The mouse is double-clicked over a particular item.
onmouseover	anything	The mouse is moved onto an item.
onmouseout	anything	The mouse moves away from an item.
onmousemove	anything	The mouse is moved while on an item.
onsubmit	Submit button	The form is submitted.
onreset	Reset button	The form is reset.

DHTML

DHTML is an acronym for *Dynamic HTML*. DHTML combines all the elements you've already learned (HTML, style sheets, and scripting) to create Web pages that are interactive and easy to update. Unfortunately,

Microsoft, Netscape, and the World Wide Web Consortium (W3C) all disagree on how to accomplish that feat. The W3C doesn't even list the acronym on their Web site discussing HTML standards.

> **Tip**   See what Microsoft has to say about DHTML at
> http://msdn.microsoft.com/workshop/author/dhtml/
> dhtmlovw.asp.
>
> You can find Netscape's description at http://
> developer.netscape.com/tech/dynhtml/.

Microsoft and Netscape do agree that DHTML should allow you to alter the appearance of a Web page after it has been loaded in the browser. They also agree that DHTML should allow developers to position any HTML element on a page. The elements can even be positioned in the same location so that, in effect, the elements appear on top of each other. But that's where the agreement ends.

Microsoft and Netscape have each developed their own browser-specific codes to achieve this type of interactivity. Using Microsoft's coding standards will mean that Netscape viewers may not be able to see the dynamic elements. The same is true if you use Netscape's coding standards. This diversity has meant that developers have been forced to choose to either ignore a whole subset of their users or to double-code all their pages to ensure that doesn't happen.

One of my favorite examples of a dynamic Web page is the Met Life Web site (www.metlife.com/). The center of the page changes depending on where I place my mouse. As Figure 14.2 shows, when I highlight the Company Info button, the center of the page tells me what type of content I'll see in the area of the Web site. When I move my mouse to another button, the center of the page changes again.

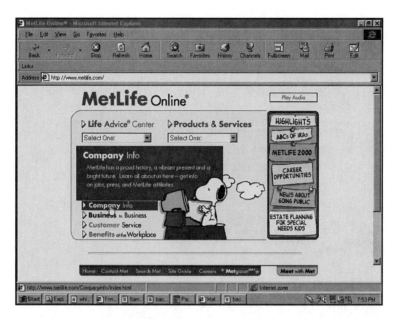

FIGURE 14.2 This Web site uses style sheets, absolute positioning, and JavaScript to dynamically alter this page.

The scope of this book does not cover all these topics in any depth, but I hope you have some idea of the possibilities and can take the time to learn more on your own. Table 14.3 lists the HTML tags that were discussed in this lesson.

TABLE 14.3 HTML Tags Used in This Lesson

HTML Tag	Closing	Description of Use
<object>	</object>	Embeds an object, such as an application, in a Web page.
<script>	</script>	Embeds a script into the Web page.

In this lesson, you've learned:

- Add Java and ActiveX applications into your HTML documents with the <object> tag.

- Add JavaScript and VBScript into your HTML documents with the <script> tag.

- DHTML combines all HTML, style sheets, and scripting to create Web pages that are interactive and easy to update.

LESSON 15

Making It Sing: Sound and Other Multimedia

In this lesson, you'll learn how to add sound and video to your Web pages, and find the plug-ins required to use them.

Adding Sound and Video

Used correctly, sound and video clips can greatly enhance the content in your Web pages. Imagine a Web page about Dr. Martin Luther King, Jr. that didn't include something about his famous "I Have a Dream" speech. The text of the speech is moving, but the delivery is what made it so powerful. You can add sound and video clips to your own Web pages using some HTML tags you've already learned.

> 💡 **Tip** You can hear samples of the "I Have a Dream" speech at www.webcorp.com/civilrights/mlkfr.htm.

Once again, however, you'll find that the three major players in the world of HTML can't agree on a method for adding something so powerful. This chapter discusses other methods for adding these sound and video clips, but the one method that is sure to work with every browser on every platform is also the simplest: the <a> tag.

```
<a href="http://www.myweb.com/sound/scream.au">Hear the
screams!</a>
```

When your visitors click on the words *Hear the screams!*, the scream.au file will download to their computers and begin playing. If the visitor does not have the right plug-in to hear the sound clip, the browser should prompt them to save the file for later. It will not, however, prompt them to download the correct plug-in. You will need to do that on your page.

Video clips can be handled in exactly the same way:

```
<a href="http://www.myweb.com/video/jumping.mpg">See the
Jumping Jack Champ in action.</a>
```

 Caution Use sound and video sparingly and make the wait worthwhile. Even short clips can have a large file size and may take a very long time to load. Make sure that you give your visitors some idea of the content of the clip so that they can decide whether to wait for the download.

<embed>

Netscape invented a new tag called <embed> to enable you to include a sound or video clip on a Web page. Microsoft's Internet Explorer browser also accepts this non-standard tag. The following sample shows how the <embed> tag works to add a video clip.

```
Want to see Rosie O'Donnell hit a hole in one? Click the video
to begin playing.
<embed src="C:\webshare\wwwroot\sams\images\holeinone.avi"
autostart="false" loop="false">
   <noembed>
   <a href="C:\webshare\wwwroot\sams\images\holeinone.avi">Click
   for a surprise.</a>
   </noembed>
</embed>
```

The browser displays a still from the video and a VCR-style push-button control, as shown in Figure 15.1. You can add width and height attributes to the <embed> tag to control the size of the video still. The <noembed> tag provides an alternate way for visitors to download the video if their browser doesn't recognize the <embed> tag.

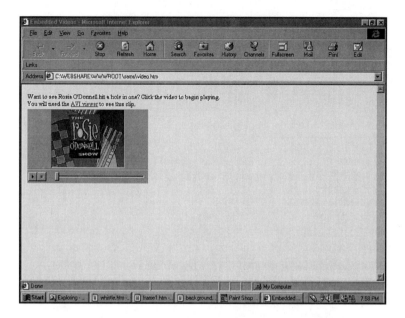

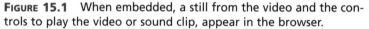

FIGURE 15.1   When embedded, a still from the video and the controls to play the video or sound clip, appear in the browser.

Notice that I've included two attributes for the <embed> tag in this example: autostart and loop. autostart, which you can set to true or false, tells the browser whether to begin playing the clip immediately upon loading the page. The loop attribute tells the browser how many times in a row to play the clip before stopping. You can set the loop attribute to any whole number.

Another attribute you can set is autorewind. This attribute is automatically set to true, but if for some reason you *don't* want to rewind the clip after it plays, you can set it to false. The hidden attribute hides the player's VCR controls from the user. Hiding the controls gives you, the developer, more control over the use of the clip, but may annoy your visitors if they are not allowed to turn your clip on or off.

`<object>`

The `<embed>` tag is non-standard, which means that the W3C doesn't recognize it as a legitimate HTML markup tag. The W3C prefers that Web page developers include sound and video clips using the `<object>` tag that you learned about in Chapter 14, "Creating Active Web Pages."

```
Want to see Rosie O'Donnell hit a hole in one? Click the video
to begin playing.<br>
<object
classid="C:\webshare\wwwroot\sams\images\holeinone.avi">
<a href="C:\webshare\wwwroot\sams\images\holeinone.avi">Click
for a surprise.</a>
</object>
```

Unfortunately, the `<object>` tag does not yet work consistently in all version 4 and higher browsers, although it is the W3C preferred tagging method. Be prepared to either always include an alternate `<a href>` tag for sound and video elements, or duplicate your work by including the `<embed>` tag as well.

The `<object>` tag, too, comes with a multitude of attributes that you can set to help control the use of the clip in your Web page. You can add a border around the object by using the `appearance` attribute and setting the value to 1. The `<object>` tag also has an `autostart` and `autorewind` attribute.

Finding Plug-ins

We've mentioned before that it's never a good idea to include any items on your Web page that require a plug-in without also providing a link to the plug-in. You don't want to assume that your visitor will have the required software to view your page because they might not.

Microsoft generally believes that the browser itself should contain enough code to run any scripts, applications, and embedded items without loading plug-ins and it uses ActiveX controls to handle these types of events. Netscape, however, agrees with the idea that browsers should be light and plug-ins should be used to handle outside events. Partially because of this belief, Netscape maintains one of the best plug-in archives on the Web at `http://home.netscape.com/plugins/index.html`.

> **Tip** If you're looking for a browser-neutral source of downloadable plug-ins, check out CNET at `www.download.com/pc/cdoor/0,323,0-60,00.html?st.dl.fd.cats.cat60.`

TABLE 15.1 HTML Tags Used in This Lesson

HTML Tag	Closing	Description of Use
`<embed>`	`</embed>`	Netscape's non-standard, although largely supported, tag for including sound and video clips.
`<noembed>`	`</noembed>`	Netscape's tag that provides an alternate method of downloading the clip for browsers that don't recognize the `<embed>` tag.
`<object>`	`</object>`	W3C's preferred, although largely *un*supported, tag for including sound and video clips.

In this lesson, you've learned:

- Sound and video clips can be added to your Web page with the `<a>` tag.

- Both the `<object>` and the `<embed>` tags enable you to add a video clip with the video controls (start, stop, and so on) to your documents.

LESSON 16

Web Page Authoring Tools

In this lesson, you'll learn where to find some of the most popular Web page authoring tools and how you can use them to create your Web site.

Why Use a Tool?

You've just spend the last fifteen chapters learning how to create Web pages by yourself, so why would you want to use a tool? The biggest reasons are time and ease of use. The Web is a very visual medium and staring at HTML code in a text editor is not very visually stimulating. It's easy to forget to be creative because you are concentrating so hard making sure that you are using the right HTML tags and putting them in the right place in the document.

Web page authoring tools come with enough bells and whistles to get your Web site started in no time. FrontPage 2000, for example, comes with 60 design themes that you can apply to your own pages to give your site a professional look. Dreamweaver has extensive support for style sheets. You can easily create style sheet declarations and apply them to the other pages in your Web site.

In the following sections, I want to introduce you to some of the most interesting features of both of these products. These two products are consistently voted as best of the best and you may find they help you, too.

Microsoft FrontPage 2000

FrontPage 2000 contains a little bit of everything. It has site management features, predesigned Web themes, starter Webs that just need your content, advanced features such as hover buttons and search bots, and all with an interface that looks like a combination of Microsoft Word and the Windows Explorer. Figure 16.1 shows a sample page in FrontPage 2000.

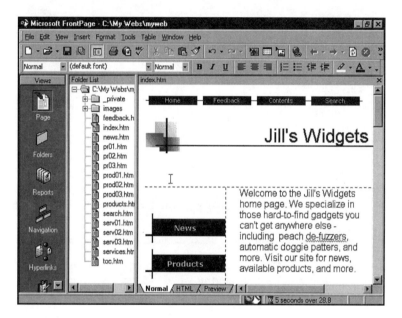

FIGURE 16.1   A sample page in FrontPage 2000.

One of the best features FrontPage has going for it, aside from the fact that the interface is so familiar to most computer users, is that it includes a variety of Web wizards you can use to define the type of site and the type of pages you want to have. Select a design theme and the program creates all your pages and adds navigation bars with the hyperlinks already in place. You just add the basic content in the middle of the page.

The Navigation view of FrontPage is exciting as well. You can add, remove, or rearrange the pages in your Web site and FrontPage automatically updates the navigation bar (see Figure 16.2).

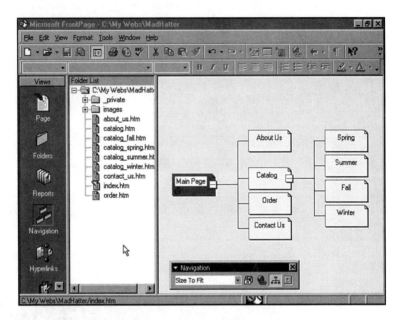

FIGURE 16.2   The Navigation view in FrontPage 2000. You can add, remove, or rearrange pages in this view and the navigation bar automatically is updated.

Packaged with the most expensive version of Office 2000, the premium package, or available separately for about $150, FrontPage integrates well with the other Microsoft Office software packages, such as Word, Excel, and Access. You can even create a Web page in Microsoft Word, save it as a Web page in your FrontPage Web site, and apply the FrontPage Web theme to the finished product without losing your original formatting.

FrontPage does support some basic database interactivity well. It can create and install an Access database from a form. In addition, extensive toolbars, menu choices, and shortcut menus make it easy to add your content without cluttering up the editing window. The tabs at the bottom of the FrontPage window enable you to see the actual HTML source code for your page (see Figure 16.3).

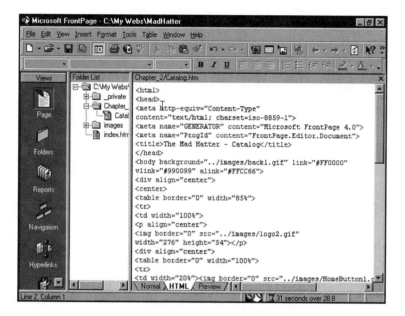

FIGURE 16.3 The HTML Source view of FrontPage 2000.

For each page, or the entire Web site, you can select the browser (Internet Explorer or Netscape) and browser version for which you want to design. If you select Netscape version 2, FrontPage will limit its feature set so that you don't inadvertently use a feature that is not supported on that particular browser.

Tip You can find out more about FrontPage 2000 at Microsoft's FrontPage Web site (www.microsoft.com/frontpage/default.htm).

FrontPage does provide some fairly advanced page components, including an ad banner manager, a hit counter, search bot, and hover buttons, as well as scheduled image and page substitutions. Most of these features, however, require FrontPage Server Extensions that you can download for free from Microsoft's site.

> **Caution** Be aware that if you create a Web site in FrontPage and want to publish it to the World Wide Web, you will need to find a Web host that supports these Server Extensions.

Macromedia Dreamweaver 2.01

Dreamweaver does not come packaged with any templates, themes, or wizards to help you get started. Nor does it feature a "looks like Microsoft Word" interface (see Figure 16.4). In fact, the interface takes some getting used to because there are floating toolbars everywhere; however, those same toolbars offer a variety of ways to enhance the pages that you create (see Figure 16.5).

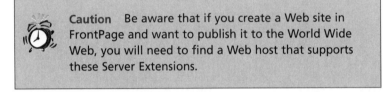

FIGURE 16.4   A sample page in Dreamweaver.

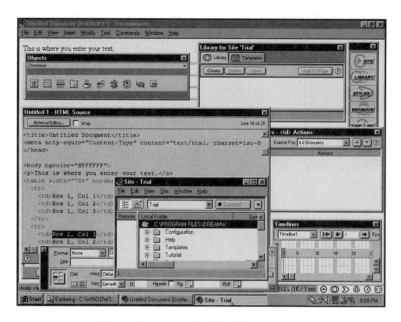

FIGURE 16.5 The same page with floating toolbars exposed.

After you design a page, you can create a template with editable and noneditable regions, which you then can use to build other pages on your site. What's more, if you change your template somewhere down the line, Dreamweaver will automatically update any page created with the template. You can use Dreamweaver's Styles window to create style sheet declarations by example and store those styles for recall in other pages (see Figure 16.6).

The Site window enables you to manage your site's content. You also can upload files into your site. Dreamweaver does not retain the formatting of imported word processor files; however, it does an excellent job of incorporating HTML files. Unlike FrontPage, however, Dreamweaver doesn't automatically create navigation bars.

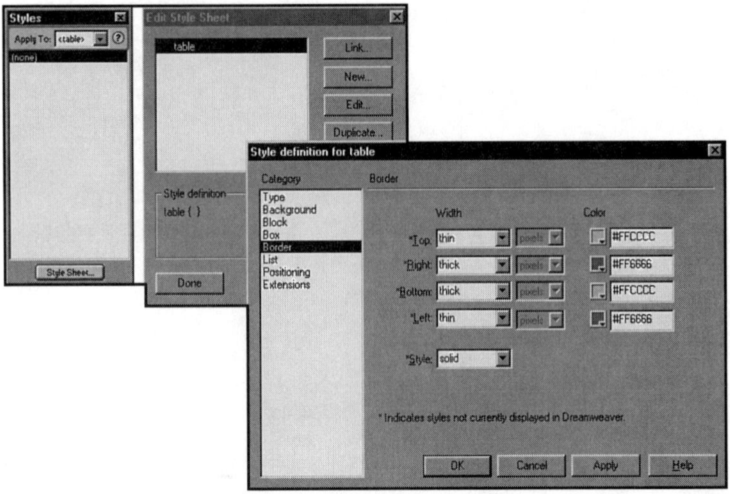

FIGURE 16.6   Style sheets are easily created and modified.

One of my favorite features is Dreamweaver's Objects palette, shown in Figure 16.7. A pop-up menu enables you to switch between the four panels described in the following list. These panels allow you to easily insert objects into your pages.

- The Common panel contains the most commonly used objects, such as images, tables, horizontal lines, layers, and multimedia objects.

- The Forms panel contains buttons for creating forms and inserting form fields.

- The Head panel contains objects for adding various <head> elements, such as the <meta> and <title> tags.

- The Invisibles panel contains buttons for creating objects that are not visible in the Document window, such as named anchors <a name="*name*"> and comments.

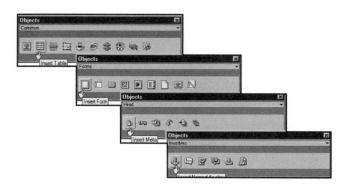

FIGURE 16.7 The Objects palette makes inserting frequently used elements easy.

Dreamweaver excels at the advanced HTML features such as layering and XML standards. Even better, because most browsers can't agree on how to support these features, Dreamweaver can check your page for compatibility with Versions 2 through 4 of both Internet Explorer and Netscape Navigator, and verify all your internal links.

Unlike FrontPage, Dreamweaver doesn't require special server extensions, or add extraneous code to your pages, which means that you'll be able to use your pages with any Web host.

Other Popular Web Tools

FrontPage and Dreamweaver aren't the only Web authoring tools available. Several more appear in the following list, along with a link to a product review from PC Computing:

- *Adobe PageMill*—www.zdnet.com/products/stories/ reviews/0,4161,402283,00.html

- *Home Page*—www.zdnet.com/products/stories/ reviews/0,4161,402285,00.html

- *HoTMetaL PRO*— www.zdnet.com/products/stories/reviews/0,4161,402286,00 .html

- *NetObjects Fusion*—www.zdnet.com/products/stories/
  reviews/0,4161,402288,00.html

- *Visual Page*—www.zdnet.com/products/stories/
  reviews/0,4161,402289,00.html

If you don't like the idea of a WYSIWYG tool and you prefer to continue working directly with the HTML source code, you probably will like HomeSite. With HomeSite, you can drag and drop HTML code, insert links, and modify existing tags. You also can search and replace HTML code, and when you're confused about which attributes apply to which tags, HomeSite can offer suggestions. All this makes HomeSite the choice of many professional developers. You can read more about HomeSite at www.allaire.com/developer/hsreferencedesk/index.cfm.

In this lesson, you've learned:

- Microsoft FrontPage is perfect for beginners. It looks like Microsoft Word and comes with many preformatted designs.

- Macromedia's Dreamweaver has advanced features, such as style sheet controls and layering, that make it perfect for professionals.

- Both tools enable you to create Web pages without knowing the HTML commands you're learning in this book.

LESSON 17

Making a Name for Yourself

In this lesson, you'll learn where to find a Web host to publish your Web site and tips for making sure your site is found.

Web Hosting

When you finally finish creating your Web pages, you're going to want to put them on the Internet and make sure they're found. Unless you plan to set up your own Web server, you'll probably be looking for a *Web hosting* service.

 Web host   A company that provides space on its Web servers to store your Web files.

Web hosting services offer a variety of services, at a variety of costs. Some Web hosts offer design services, customizable scripts, visitor logs, database support, and more, in addition to the standard disk space. Use the information in Table 17.1 to find a Web host that meets your needs.

TABLE 17.1   Web Hosting Resources

Host Name	Comments	URL
The List	The official list of Internet Service Providers	`thelist.internet.com`
Web Host Power Search	Find a Web host by selecting from a feature list	`www.internetlist.com/screens/search/hostsearch.asp`
Yahoo!Geocities	Free Web hosting with authoring resources	`geocities.yahoo.com/home/`
Tripod	Free Web hosting	`www.tripod.com`
Cybercities	Free Web hosting	`www.cybercities.com`
Register FrontPage Hosts	Web hosts that support Microsoft FrontPage, and who have registered with Microsoft	`www.microsoftwpp.com/wppsearch/`

Search Pages and Indexes

After your HTML documents are up and running on a Web server, you'll need to make sure that people can find them. Because most people look to *search engines* when they want to find something on the Internet, we'll start there.

 Search engines   Searchable indexes of Web resources. Some search engines (called indexes) also categorize the information to enable people to search by categories, as well as using keywords.

Two types of search engines exist on the Web: spiders and indexes.

* A *spider* (also called a Web crawler, or *bot* which is short for
robot) is an automated script that crawls through Web pages following hyperlinks to find related pages and then builds a database of the contents of all the pages it visits.

* A *search index* is an automated script that looks in a pre-
populated database for pages containing specific words or
phrases. The search index's administrative personnel review the
content of the pages and populate the database.

Search Bots

Search engine bots (also called robots, spiders, and crawlers) will search
through all Web pages and then index them according to the information
they find. You can help the indexing portion be more accurate by using
<meta> tags. Without <meta> tags, these bots treat every word in a docu-
ment exactly alike. If you add keywords and descriptions to your documents, you'll increase the possibility that your Web pages will be found.
You learned how to do this in Chapter 9, "Even More Tags," but let's try a
quick refresher. The following example shows you the correct format for
adding the <meta> tag to your documents. Figure 17.1 is an actual example of the <meta> tags used on the WebReference.com site.

```
<html lang="en-US">
<head>
<title>Your HTML Page</title>
<meta name="keywords" contents="keywords that people like use
to search for your page.">
<meta name="description" contents="a brief paragraph describ-
ing your document.">
<meta name="author" contents="your name">
</head>
<style type="text/css">
</style>
<body>
    insert your document here.
</body>
</html>
```

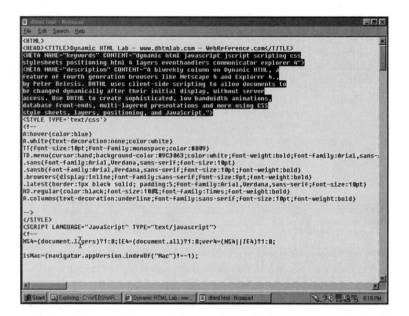

FIGURE 17.1 The HTML source code for http://webreference. com/dhtml/ with the <meta> tags highlighted.

> Tip   Try adding your competitors' names to your
> keyword list. That way when people are looking for
> your competitor, your name will show in their list.

Adding Your Web Site to the Search Engine

All search engines enable Web authors to add the URL of their own Web
site to the search engine. Most of them do this with some type of online
form. A link to Yahoo!'s Suggest a Site form appears at the bottom of

every Yahoo! Page (see Figures 17.2 and 17.3). Yahoo! requires you to find the appropriate category for your Web page before submitting the site. In this way, Yahoo! adds the category information to the rest of the information that you enter to help rank your pages.

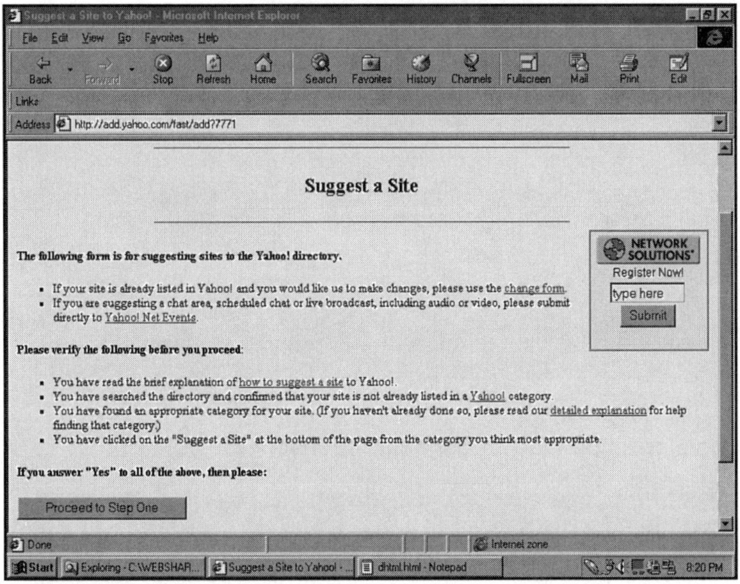

FIGURE 17.2   Yahoo!'s Suggest a Site page enables you to add your Web page to the Yahoo! index.

The Add URL form on Excite's search engine page asks only for the URL of your home page and a simple category (see Figure 17.4). Other search engines require similar information before adding your site to their list.

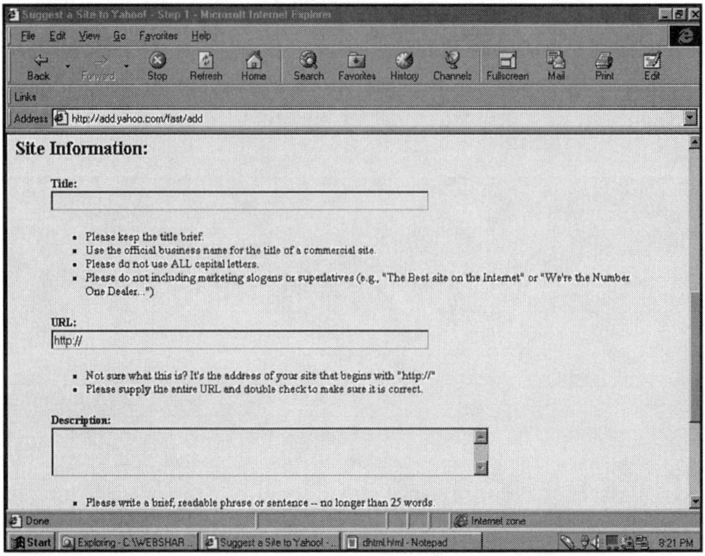

FIGURE 17.3 Yahoo!'s Suggest a Site form allows you to control the description that Yahoo! displays for your Web site.

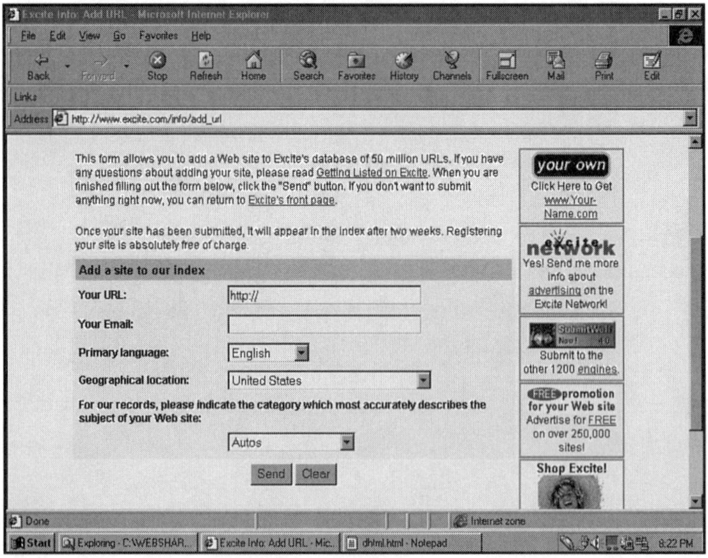

FIGURE 17.4 Excite's Add URL form.

Tip   Some Web sites offer to add your URL to many (if not all) search sites with one form. Companies such as www.submit-it.com and www.liquidimaging.com /submit/ are popular examples. Go ahead and use these (if you are willing to pay the fee associated). However, you'll probably want to add your own site information to the most popular search sites (Yahoo!, eXcite, AltaVista, Lycos, InfoSeek, and the latest, Go.com) to assure yourself the best chance of being found.

Advertising

Don't forget that you can advertise on the Web too. The following list of Web sites offer some form of advertising or announcement service. The flashy banner ads that proliferate the Web are there for a reason: people actually click on them. These advertising services can help you create your own ad and place it on pages that relate to your site.

- http://dir.yahoo.com/Computers_and_Internet/ Internet/World_Wide_Web/Announcement_Services/

- www.smartage.com/excite_clicks/

- www.banneradnetwork.com

Tip   Remember to include your URL on your business cards, letterhead, and email auto-signature. Unless you tell people where to look, they won't find you.

In this lesson, you've learned:

- Two types of search engines exist on the Web: spiders and indexes.

- Add keywords for the search engines with <meta> tags. Different search engines search for different <meta> tags, so use several including keywords, description, and author.

- Most search engines have their own site-submittal forms. Fill out these forms so that the search engine can find your site.

LESSON 18

XML and the Future of the Internet

In this lesson, you'll learn what's next for the Internet and what you can do now to prepare for the coming changes.

The Future of the Internet

The extraordinary growth of the Internet since the early 1990s has come about chiefly because HTML is so easy to learn. Companies can distribute information to their employees, customers, and business partners quickly and inexpensively. Unfortunately, or fortunately depending on your point of view, the first blush of Internet and Web development has passed and companies are already beginning to look for new ways to disseminate the information that they want to share.

Hearing this cry for help, the World Wide Web Consortium has developed an eXtensible Markup Language (XML) that can be used by those Web page authors whose needs extend beyond the capabilities of HTML.

 eXtensible Markup Language (XML) The newest language being developed by the World Wide Web Consortium. It is more flexible than HTML.

What Is XML?

To understand XML, you need to step back and remember what HTML is. HTML is a markup language that uses a predefined set of tags to describe a document's structure in terms of paragraphs, headings, meta information, and so on. XML takes tagging one step further. Rather than the structure of a document, with XML, we use tags to add meaning to any word in the paragraph. Both markup languages use style sheets to define the format of each tag with color, fonts, and emphasis.

I can hear you, you know. You're wondering why on earth you would ever want to "add meaning to a word." After all, you're not a dictionary, and how could you possibly learn all those tags. It's not as hard as you think. The following examples show how a single line from a nursery rhyme might be marked up in both HTML and XML, respectively.

- HTML:

    ```
    <p>Little Bo Peep has lost her sheep.<p>
    ```

- XML:

    ```
    <girl><name>Little Bo Peep</name></girl> has
    <disposition>lost</disposition>her
    <animal><wool_source>sheep</wool_source></animal>.
    ```

With HTML, any word in the sentence holds the same weight as the next word and there is no context to the words in the sentence. In the XML example, nearly every word has some type of description surrounding it. Okay, why is that important? Because, in essence, your document becomes a giant database of information you can share with anyone.

Suppose that I am the owner of a chain of multiplex theaters and I want to put information on the Web about the movies I'm showing. In traditional Web publishing (if something as young as the World Wide Web can be said to even have a traditional method), I could do one of the following two things.

- Create a series of Web pages that would need to be updated frequently.

- Create a database that held all the information and then hire a Java programmer to write an application that would enable people to perform searches on my database to see what was showing in their neighborhood.

With the advent of XML, I have a third option. I can create a single Web page that contains all the information for all my theaters and use style sheets and templates to present the right information to the right people. Because the standard isn't finished, I won't spend the time to tell you how to create XML documents, but I will talk you through each of the elements so that you have a better understanding.

Analyze the Data

The first thing I have to do is analyze my data. What information do I need to share? I probably would want to share the name of the movie, a brief description, the names of the stars in the movie, links to promotional information for the film, the name of the theater in which it's playing, the address of the theater, my phone number, the time the movie is showing, the price of the movie, whether discounts are accepted, and probably a lot more.

After you know the type of data you need to collect, you can create your XML input document. You can see an example of two of these input documents in Figure 18.1. Each data type is represented by a pair of tags (such as `<movie>` and `</movie>`). Related data types are nested within a parent tag: the `<title>` and `<star>` tags are related to the `<movie>` tag, for example. Unlike HTML, I made up my own XML tags based on the information I wanted to present.

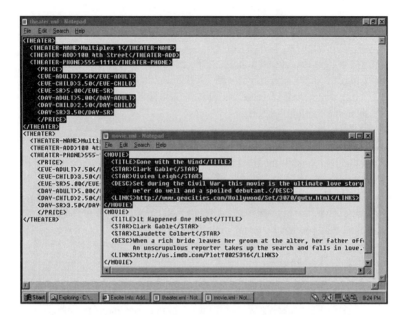

FIGURE 18.1 An XML input document defines the data for each XML tag.

> **Caution** Don't rush out to convert all your HTML documents yet. The W3C is still working on its recommendations for the XML standard. Many of the final decisions, with regard to linking capability and style sheet templates, haven't been completed yet. Only Microsoft's Internet Explorer 5 includes any type of XML viewing support with Netscape Navigator close behind.

Create a Style Sheet Template

After you complete the input document, you will need to create a style sheet template that determines how you will present your information. You can think of the style sheet template as a combination of HTML document and a style sheet. The template defines the structure of the document (tables, lists, paragraphs, and so on), and the style sheet elements define the look of the elements.

The real fun with XML documents comes from the fact that the content of the page is separated from its format. In the movie theater example, suppose that I own two movie theaters. Multiplex 1 is a downtown art theater (refer to Figure 18.1). It only shows artsy films that serious film students attend and it likes to promote itself as a dark, almost somber environment. Multiplex 2 is in a posh part of uptown and shows mostly revivals to an older, more conservative crowd. Now imagine that I'm planning to show the same movie, *Citizen Kane*, at both theaters.

My input document, which holds the content that will appear on the Web site for both theaters, would include the following tags for *Citizen Kane*:

```
<movie>
   <title>Citizen Kane</title>
   <star>Orson Wells</star>
   <desc>Powerful newspaper owner Charles Foster Kane was many
   things to many people,both in life and, as seen in
   retrospective, in death.</desc>
   <links>http://us.imdb.com/Tawards?0033467</links>
</movie>
```

Using style sheet templates, I can create two completely different pages for my theaters. For Multiplex 1, the artsy theater, I might choose to have a black background with the title in a dramatic gothic-looking font and the other elements (star, desc, and links) placed in a bulleted list below.

For Multiplex 2, the revival theater, I might create a background image of a film canister for my page. I then might choose to place all the elements of the movie into a horizontal table for a more conservative feel.

I can do that because style sheet templates do not reference the actual content items. Rather than placing the content (*Citizen Kane*) on the style sheet template, I would place the following tag, which tells your computer to insert the information in the <title> tag.

```
<xsl:value-of select="title"/>
```

Tip   You can learn more about XML from the W3C at www.w3.org/XML/. Another excellent resource for XML information is the What the ?XML! Web site at www.geocities.com/SiliconValley/Peaks/5957/xml.html.

XML promises to be a platform-independent, software-independent language. Web developers and other programmers will be able to use the same data input documents to present information over the Web, in business automation tools (such as spreadsheets and word processors), and even on paper. That can save all of us a lot of time and money.

Planning for the Future

More and more, computer application developers are choosing to create their applications using Web technology. Whereas just 10 years ago, schools were busy teaching their students how to write BASIC programs and type DOS commands at the appropriate prompts, now they are teaching students HTML, and learning to browse the Internet is a requirement.

Some schools even offer homework help over the Internet. The Internet and Web technology is not going away and it is going to continue to grow and change. That's why it is important to understand what you can do now to make sure that you aren't caught off guard the next time the standard changes.

Check Your Code

Microsoft, and Netscape, the two largest competitors in the browser wars, continue to try to outdo each other with new browser features. Both browsers have been known to create new commands that work only on their own browsers. If you use those commands when you are creating your Web site, you will end up forcing your viewers to choose a browser, or lose important features that you intended to share with them. Don't put them in that position. You can use tools such as Web Site Garage's TuneUp (`http://websitegarage.netscape.com/0=wsg/tuneup_plus/index.html`) to ensure that your site is the best it can be.

Be sure to test your pages on different browsers and older browser versions—not everyone will be using the newest version of the browser and some older versions do not support as many tags. The Browser Snapshot feature at the Web Site Garage can do this for you, for a small fee. Figure 18.2 shows what you can expect from their service. Above the browser screenshot, Web Site Garage tells you which browser (and at what resolution) the screen shot was taken.

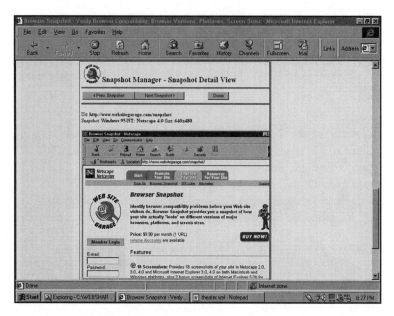

Figure 18.2   The Web Site Garage can test your pages for browser compatibility.

Use Correct Syntax

HTML is a very forgiving language. It knows, for example, that although you forgot to close your `<li>` (list item) tag within a `<ul>` (unordered, or bulleted, list), when you added the next `<li>` tag you want the last one to close. To HTML, the following:

```
<ul>
<li>One ring-y, ding-y
<li>Two ring-y, ding-ys
</ul>
```

is the same as this:

```
<UL>
<LI>One ring-y, ding-y</LI>
<LI>Two ring-y, ding-ys</LI>
</UL>
```

and the same as this:

```
<ul>
<Li>One ring-y, ding-y</Li>
<LI>Two ring-y, ding-ys</li>
</Ul>
```

Notice, too, that capitalization of the tags is irrelevant in HTML; XML requires that all tags be lowercase.

Unfortunately, this forgiving attitude may not always be true. As the W3C moves ever closer to XML, with which we will be able to create our own tags, more structure will be required to differentiate between those tags. Learn now to use the proper syntax for your documents and you won't find yourself reworking your documents later.

Use Style Sheets

In previous versions of HTML, Web page authors controlled the color, format, and layout of their documents with formatting tags such as `<font color="color" size="size" family="font name">` and `<body bgcolor="color">`. With HTML 4, the W3C is recommending that all these format attributes are controlled with style sheets instead.

This book has focused on the HTML 4 preferences, which may mean that older browsers don't always see what you intended. You can add older HTML tags to your documents without affecting your style sheets, as shown in Figure 18.3. Just remember that the HTML format tags and the style sheet properties cannot conflict, or you will find problems. If your style sheet property tells the browser that the <body> tag should have a yellow background, for example, be sure that the <body> tag also calls for a yellow background. If you do choose conflicting attributes by mistake, the style sheet property will take precedence.

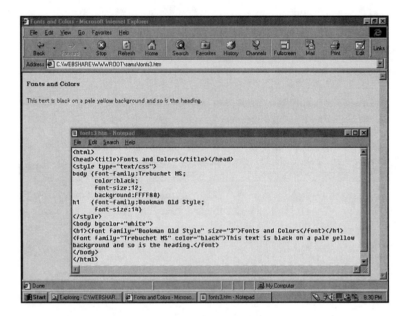

FIGURE 18.3   The HTML document seen in Figure 10.2 now has formatting tags added for older browsers.

Nest Tags Properly

Because HTML and XML are becoming more structured, it will do you well to get into the habit of paying attention to the details. You've seen in previous chapters that you can "nest" one HTML tag inside another.

If you want to have text within a table cell (or any tagged element, such as a <ul>, <li>, and so on) to be both bold and italic, remember to close the tags in the order that you opened them. The following example shows that <b> was opened first and closed last.

```
<table>
<tr>
<td>
<b><i>This is bold and italicized text.</i></b>
</td>
</tr>
</table>
```

You might nest tags within a paragraph, as shown in the following example. The first two sentences are both bold, although only the second is italicized. Remember to add the second <i> tag. You'll be glad you did when HTML and the browsers require it.

```
<b>This text is bold.<i>This is bold and
italicized.</i></b><i>This is just italicized.</i>
```

Check It Twice

It's such a simple thing that we often overlook it, but your pages will appear more professional and your visitors will have more respect for the information you provide, if your content is spelled correctly.

By the same token, don't publish broken links. Nothing is worse than clicking on a link that goes nowhere, or leads to the dreaded 404 error. Make sure you verify that all your links go where you want them to go.

Learn All You Can

The Internet is a great place to learn about HTML, XML, and the World Wide Web. Check out some of the following great resources.

- *W3C's HTML 4.0 Specification*—www.w3.org/MarkUp/

- *W3C's XML 1.0 Recommendation*—www.w3.org/XML/

- *XML, Java, and the Future of the Web*—http://metalab.
  unc.edu/pub/sun-info/standards/xml/why/xmlapps.htm

- *XML Resource Guide*—www.xml.com/xml/pub/listrescat

- *CNET's Spotlight on XML*—
  www.builder.com/Authoring/XmlSpot/?tag=st.cn.sr1.ssr.
  bl_xml

In this lesson, you've learned:

- XML goes beyond HTML. Rather than just assigning a structure to the text (with paragraph, headings, tables, and so on), XML adds meaning and order.

- The XML standard isn't complete yet, but it will take over the Internet as soon as it is.

- There are things you can do now to ensure that you are ready for the future of the Internet: use the correct syntax for all commands, use lowercase HTML commands, nest your tags appropriately, and use style sheets rather than the HTML formatting codes.

APPENDIX A

HTML 4 Quick Reference

HTML 4 is an ambitious attempt to meet the needs of Web developers worldwide, both casual and professional. XHTML 1 is a reformulation of HTML 4 as an XML 1 application, allowing extensions to the language to be more easily defined and implemented. This appendix provides a quick reference to most of the elements and attributes of HTML 4/XHTML 1.

> **Note** This appendix is based on the information provided in the *HTML 4.0 Specification W3C Recommendation*, revised on April 24, 1998, and the *XHTML 1.0 Specification Working Draft*, revised on May 5, 1999. The latest versions of these standards can be found at http://www.w3.org/.

To make the information readily accessible, this appendix organizes HTML elements by their function in the following order:

- Structure
- Text phrases and paragraphs
- Text font elements
- Lists
- Links
- Tables

- Frames
- Embedded content
- Style
- Forms
- Scripts

The elements are listed alphabetically within each section, and the following information is presented:

- Usage—A general description of the element
- Start/End Tag—Indicates whether these tags are required, optional, or illegal
- Attributes—Lists the attributes of the element with a short description of their effect
- Empty—Indicates whether the element can be empty
- Notes—Relates any special considerations when using the element and indicates whether the element is new, deprecated, or obsolete

 deprecate   Several elements and attributes have been *deprecated*, which means they have been outdated by the current HTML version, and you should avoid using them. The same or similar functionality is provided by using new features.

Following this, the common attributes and intrinsic events are summarized.

Note   HTML 4 introduces several new attributes that apply to a significant number of elements. These are referred to within each element listing as core, i18n, and events.

Structure

HTML relies on several elements to provide structure to a document (as opposed to structuring the text within) as well as provide information that is used by the browser or search engines.

> **Note** There are, in fact, three versions ("Document Type Definitions" or "DTDs") of HTML 4: Strict (pure HTML 4), Transitional (elements within the Strict DTD plus additional elements held over from HTML 3.2), and Frameset (Transitional plus frames). Each one relies upon a DTD to specify which elements and attributes are to be used, and the DTD is noted here.

<body>...</body>

Usage	Contains the document's content.
Start/End Tag	Optional/Optional.
Attributes	core, i18n, events.

background="..." Deprecated. URL for the background image.

bgcolor="..." Deprecated. Sets background color.

text="..." Deprecated. Text color.

link="..." Deprecated. Link color.

vlink="..." Deprecated. Visited link color.

alink="..." Deprecated. Active link color.

onload="..." Intrinsic event triggered when the document loads.

onunload="..."   Intrinsic event triggered
when document unloads.

Empty   No.

Notes   Strict DTD. There can be only one <body>,
                 and it must follow the <head>. The <body>
                 element can be replaced by a <frameset> ele-
                 ment. The presentational attributes are depre-
                 cated in favor of setting these values with
                 style sheets.

Comments <! – ... – >

Usage   Used to insert notes or scripts that are not dis-
                 played by the browser.

Start/End Tag   Required/Required.

Attributes   None.

Empty   Yes.

Notes   Comments are not restricted to one line and
                 can be any length. The end tag is not required
                 to be on the same line as the start tag.

<div>...</div>

Usage   The division element is used to add structure
                 to a block of text.

Start/End Tag   Required/Required.

Attributes   core, i18n, events.

                 align="..."   Deprecated. Controls align-
                 ment (left, center, right, justify).

Empty   No.

Notes   Strict DTD. Cannot be used within a P ele-
                 ment. The align attribute is deprecated in
                 favor of controlling alignment through style
                 sheets.

> **Note**   You will notice that the oft-used align
> attribute has been deprecated. This affects a large
> number of elements whose rendered position was
> controlled by setting the alignment to a suitable
> value, such as right or center. Also deprecated is the
> <center> element. The W3C strongly encourages users
> to begin using style sheets to modify the visual for-
> matting of an HTML document.

<!doctype...>

Usage   Version information appears on the first line
                 of an HTML document and is an SGML dec-
                 laration rather than an element.

<h1>...</h1> through <h6>...</h6>

Usage   The six headings (h1 is uppermost, or most
                 important) are used in the body to structure
                 information in a hierarchical fashion.

Start/End Tag   Required/Required.

Attributes   core, i18n, events.

                 align="..."   Deprecated. Controls align-
                 ment (left, center, right, justify).

Empty	No.
Notes	Strict DTD. Visual browsers will display the size of the headings in relation to their importance, <h1> being the largest and <h6> the smallest. The align attribute is deprecated in favor of controlling alignment through style sheets.

<head>...</head>

Usage	This is the document header and contains other elements that provide information to users and search engines.
Start/End Tag	Optional/Optional.
Attributes	i18n.
	profile="..." URL specifying the location of meta data.
Empty	No.
Notes	Strict DTD. There can be only one <head> per document. It must follow the opening <html> tag and precede the <body>.

<hr />

Usage	Horizontal rules are used to separate sections of a Web page.
Start/End Tag	Required/Illegal.
Attributes	core, events.
	align="..." Deprecated. Controls alignment (left, center, right, justify).

noshade="..."   Displays the rule as a solid color.

size="..."   Deprecated. The size of the rule.

width="..."   Deprecated. The width of the rule.

Empty   Yes.

Notes   Strict DTD.

`<html>...</html>`

Usage   The html element contains the entire document.

Start/End Tag   Optional/Optional.

Attributes   i18n.

version="..."   URL of the document type definition specifying the HTML version used to create the document.

Empty   No.

Notes   Strict DTD. The version information is duplicated in the `<!doctype...>` declaration and is therefore not essential.

`<meta />`

Usage   Provides information about the document.

Start/End Tag   Required/Illegal.

Attributes   i18n.

`http-equiv="..."` HTTP response header name.

`name="..."` Name of the `meta` information.

`content="..."` Content of the `meta` information.

`scheme="..."` Assigns a scheme to interpret the `meta` data.

Empty	Yes.
Notes	Strict DTD.

`<title>...</title>`

Usage	This is the name you give your Web page. The `<title>` element is located in the `<head>` element and is displayed in the browser window title bar.
Start/End Tag	Required/Required.
Attributes	`i18n`.
Empty	No.
Notes	Strict DTD. Only one title allowed per document.

Text Phrases and Paragraphs

Text phrases (or blocks) can be structured to suit a specific purpose, such as creating a paragraph. This should not be confused with modifying the formatting of the text.

`<address>...</address>`

Usage	Provides a special format for author or contact information.
Start/End Tag	Required/Required.
Attributes	`core, i18n, events.`
Empty	No.
Notes	Strict DTD. The ` ` element is commonly used inside the `<address>` element to break the lines of an address.

`<blockquote>...</blockquote>`

Usage	Used to display long quotations.
Start/End Tag	Required/Required.
Attributes	`core, i18n, events.`
	`cite="..."` The URL of the quoted text.
Empty	No.
Notes	Strict DTD.

`<br />`

Usage	Forces a line break.
Start/End Tag	Required/Illegal.
Attributes	`core, i18n, events.`
	`clear="..."` Sets the location where next line begins after a floating object (`none`, `left`, `right`, `all`).
Empty	Yes.
Notes	Strict DTD.

`<em>...</em>`

Usage	Emphasized text.
Start/End Tag	Required/Required.
Attributes	core, i18n, events.
Empty	No.
Notes	Strict DTD.

`<p>...</p>`

Usage	Defines a paragraph.
Start/End Tag	Required/Optional.
Attributes	core, i18n, events.
	align="..." Deprecated. Controls alignment (left, center, right, justify).
Empty	No.
Notes	Strict DTD.

`<pre>...</pre>`

Usage	Displays preformatted text.
Start/End Tag	Required/Required.
Attributes	core, i18n, events.
	width="..." The width of the formatted text.
Empty	No.
Notes	Strict DTD.

`<strong>...</strong>`

Usage	Stronger emphasis.
Start/End Tag	Required/Required.
Attributes	`core, i18n, events.`
Empty	No.
Notes	Strict DTD.

`<sub>...</sub>`

Usage	Creates subscript.
Start/End Tag	Required/Required.
Attributes	`core, i18n, events.`
Empty	No.
Notes	Strict DTD.

`<sup>...</sup>`

Usage	Creates superscript.
Start/End Tag	Required/Required.
Attributes	`core, i18n, events.`
Empty	No.
Notes	Strict DTD.

Text Formatting Elements

Text characteristics such as the size, weight, and style can be modified using these elements, but the HTML 4 specification encourages you to use style sheets instead.

`<b>...</b>`

Usage	Bold text.
Start/End Tag	Required/Required.
Attributes	`core, i18n, events`.
Empty	No.
Notes	Strict DTD.

`<big>...</big>`

Usage	Large text.
Start/End Tag	Required/Required.
Attributes	`core, i18n, events`.
Empty	No.
Notes	Strict DTD.

`<font>...</font>`

Usage	Changes the font size and color.
Start/End Tag	Required/Required.
Attributes	`size="..."` The font size (1 through 7 or relative, which is +3).
	`color="..."` The font color.
	`face="..."` The font type.
Empty	No.
Notes	Transitional DTD. Deprecated in favor of style sheets.

`<i>...</i>`

Usage	Italicized text.
Start/End Tag	Required/Required.
Attributes	core, i18n, events.
Empty	No.
Notes	Strict DTD.

`<s>...</s>`

Usage	Strikethrough text.
Start/End Tag	Required/Required.
Attributes	core, i18n, events.
Empty	No.
Notes	Transitional DTD. Deprecated.

`<small>...</small>`

Usage	Small text.
Start/End Tag	Required/Required.
Attributes	core, i18n, events.
Empty	No.
Notes	Strict DTD.

`<tt>...</tt>`

Usage	Teletype (or monospaced) text.
Start/End Tag	Required/Required.
Attributes	core, i18n, events.

Empty	No.
Notes	Strict DTD.

`<u>...</u>`

Usage	Underlined text.
Start/End Tag	Required/Required.
Attributes	`core, i18n, events`.
Empty	No.
Notes	Transitional DTD. Deprecated.

Lists

You can organize text into a more structured outline by creating lists. Lists can be nested.

`<dd>...</dd>`

Usage	The definition description used in a `<dl>` (definition list) element.
Start/End Tag	Required/Optional.
Attributes	`core, i18n, events`.
Empty	No.
Notes	Strict DTD. Can contain block-level content, such as the `<p>` element.

`<dir>...</dir>`

Usage	Creates a multi-column directory list.
Start/End Tag	Required/Required.

Attributes	`core`, `i18n`, `events`.
	`compact="compact"` Deprecated. Compacts the displayed list.
Empty	No.
Notes	Transitional DTD. Must contain at least one list item. This element is deprecated in favor of the `<ul>` (unordered list) element.

`<dl>...</dl>`

Usage	Creates a definition list.
Start/End Tag	Required/Required.
Attributes	`core`, `i18n`, `events`.
	`compact="compact"` Deprecated. Compacts the displayed list.
Empty	No.
Notes	Strict DTD. Must contain at least one `<dt>` or `<dd>` element in any order.

`<dt>...</dt>`

Usage	The definition term (or label) used within a `<dl>` (definition list) element.
Start/End Tag	Required/Optional.
Attributes	`core`, `i18n`, `events`.
Empty	No.
Notes	Strict DTD. Must contain text (which can be modified by text mark-up elements).

`<li>...</li>`

Usage	Defines a list item within a list.
Start/End Tag	Required/Optional.
Attributes	core, i18n, events.
	type="..." Changes the numbering style (1, a, A, i, I), ordered lists, or bullet style (disc, square, circle) in unordered lists.
	value="..." Sets the numbering to the given integer beginning with the current list item.
Empty	No.
Notes	Strict DTD.

`<ol>...</ol>`

Usage	Creates an ordered list.
Start/End Tag	Required/Required.
Attributes	core, i18n, events.
	type="..." Sets the numbering style (1, a, A, i, I).
	compact Deprecated. Compacts the displayed list.
	start="..." Sets the starting number to the chosen integer.
Empty	No.
Notes	Strict DTD. Must contain at least one list item.

`<ul>...</ul>`

Usage	Creates an unordered list.
Start/End Tag	Required/Required.
Attributes	`core, i18n, events`.
	`type="..."` Sets the bullet style (`disc`, `square`, `circle`).
	`compact="compact"` Deprecated. Compacts the displayed list.
Empty	No.
Notes	Strict DTD. Must contain at least one list item.

Links

Hyperlinking is fundamental to HTML. These elements enable you to link to other documents, other locations within a document, or external files.

`<A>...</A>`

Usage	Used to define links and anchors.
Start/End Tag	Required/Required.
Attributes	`core, i18n, events`.
	`charset="..."` Character encoding of the resource.
	`name="..."` Defines an anchor.
	`href="..."` The URL of the linked resource.

`target="..."` Determines where the resource will be displayed (user-defined name, `_blank`, `_parent`, `_self`, `_top`).

`rel="..."` Forward link types.

`rev="..."` Reverse link types.

`accesskey="..."` Assigns a hotkey to this element.

`shape="..."` Enables you to define client-side imagemaps using defined shapes (`default`, `rect`, `circle`, `poly`).

`coords="..."` Sets the size of the shape using pixel or percentage lengths.

`tabindex="..."` Sets the tabbing order between elements with a defined `tabindex`.

Empty   No.

Notes   Strict DTD.

Tables

Tables are meant to display data in a tabular format. Before the introduction of HTML 4, tables were widely used for page layout purposes, but with the advent of style sheets, this is being discouraged by the W3C.

`<caption>...</caption>`

Usage   Displays a table caption.

Start/End Tag Required/Required.

Attributes   `core`, `i18n`, `events`.

`align="..."` Deprecated. Controls alignment (`left`, `center`, `right`, `justify`).

Empty	No.
Notes	Strict DTD. Optional.

`<table>...</table>`

Usage	Creates a table.
Start/End Tag	Required/Required.
Attributes	`core`, `i18n`, `events`.
	`align="..."` Deprecated. Controls alignment (`left`, `center`, `right`, `justify`).
	`bgcolor="..."` Deprecated. Sets the background color.
	`width="..."` Table width.
	`cols="..."` The number of columns.
	`border="..."` The width in pixels of a border around the table.
	`frame="..."` Sets the visible sides of a table (`void`, `above`, `below`, `hsides`, `lhs`, `rhs`, `vsides`, `box`, `border`).
	`rules="..."` Sets the visible rules within a table (`none`, `groups`, `rows`, `cols`, `all`).
	`cellspacing="..."` Spacing between cells.
	`cellpadding="..."` Spacing in cells.
Empty	No.
Notes	Strict DTD.

`<td>...</td>`

Usage	Defines a cell's contents.
Start/End Tag	Required/Optional.
Attributes	`core`, `i18n`, `events`.

`axis="..."` Abbreviated name.

`axes="..."` axis names listing row and column headers pertaining to the cell.

`nowrap="..."` Deprecated. Turns off text wrapping in a cell.

`bgcolor="..."` Deprecated. Sets the background color.

`rowspan="..."` The number of rows spanned by a cell.

`colspan="..."` The number of columns spanned by a cell.

`align="..."` Horizontally aligns the contents of cells (`left`, `center`, `right`, `justify`, `char`).

`char="..."` Sets a character on which the column aligns.

`charoff="..."` Offset to the first alignment character on a line.

`valign="..."` Vertically aligns the contents of cells (`top`, `middle`, `bottom`, `baseline`).

Empty	No.
Notes	Strict DTD.

`<th>...</th>`

Usage	Defines the cell contents of the table header.
Start/End Tag	Required/Optional.
Attributes	`core`, `i18n`, `events`.

`axis="..."`   Abbreviated name.

`axes="..."`   axis names listing row and column headers pertaining to the cell.

`nowrap="..."`   Deprecated. Turns off text wrapping in a cell.

`bgcolor="..."`   Deprecated. Sets the background color.

`rowspan="..."`   The number of rows spanned by a cell.

`colspan="..."`   The number of columns spanned by a cell.

`align="..."`   Horizontally aligns the contents of cells (`left`, `center`, `right`, `justify`, `char`).

`char="..."`   Sets a character on which the column aligns.

`charoff="..."`   Offset to the first alignment character on a line.

`valign="..."`   Vertically aligns the contents of cells (`top`, `middle`, `bottom`, `baseline`).

Empty	No.
Notes	Strict DTD.

`<tr>...</tr>`

Usage	Defines a row of table cells.
Start/End Tag	Required/Optional.
Attributes	`core`, `i18n`, `events`.
	`align="..."` Horizontally aligns the contents of cells (`left`, `center`, `right`, `justify`, `char`).
	`char="..."` Sets a character on which the column aligns.
	`charoff="..."` Offset to the first alignment character on a line.
	`valign="..."` Vertically aligns the contents of cells (`top`, `middle`, `bottom`, `baseline`).
	`bgcolor="..."` Deprecated. Sets the background color.
Empty	No.
Notes	Strict DTD.

Frames

Frames create new "panels" in the Web browser window that are used to display content from different source documents.

`<frame />`

Usage	Defines a frame.
Start/End Tag	Required/Illegal.
Attributes	`name="..."` The name of a frame.
	`src="..."` The source to be displayed in a frame.

frameborder="..." Toggles the border between frames (0, 1).

marginwidth="..." Sets the space between the frame border and content.

marginheight="..." Sets the space between the frame border and content.

noresize Disables sizing.

scrolling="..." Determines scrollbar presence (auto, yes, no).

Empty	Yes.
Notes	Frameset DTD. This element is new to HTML 4.

<frameset>...</frameset>

Usage	Defines the layout of frames within a window.
Start/End Tag	Required/Required.
Attributes	rows="..." The number of rows.
	cols="..." The number of columns.
	onload="..." The intrinsic event triggered when the document loads.
	onunload="..." The intrinsic event triggered when the document unloads.
Empty	No.
Notes	Frameset DTD. This element is new to HTML 4. Framesets can be nested.

`<iframe>...</iframe>`

Usage	Creates an inline frame.
Start/End Tag	Required/Required.
Attributes	`name="..."` The name of the frame.
	`src="..."` The source to be displayed in a frame.
	`frameborder="..."` Toggles the border between frames (`0`, `1`).
	`marginwidth="..."` Sets the space between the frame border and content.
	`marginheight="..."` Sets the space between the frame border and content.
	`scrolling="..."` Determines scrollbar presence (`auto`, `yes`, `no`).
	`align="..."` Deprecated. Controls alignment (`left`, `center`, `right`, `justify`).
	`height="..."` Height.
	`width="..."` Width.
Empty	No.
Notes	Transitional DTD. This element is new to HTML 4.

`<noframes>...</noframes>`

Usage	Alternative content when frames are not supported.
Start/End Tag	Required/Required.
Attributes	None.

Empty	No.
Notes	Frameset DTD. This element is new to HTML 4.

Embedded Content

> **embedded content** Also called *inclusions*, embedded content applies to Java applets, imagemaps, and other multimedia or programmed content that is placed in a Web page to provide additional functionality.

`<applet>...</applet>`

Usage	Includes a Java applet.
Start/End Tag	Required/Required.
Attributes	`codebase="..."` The URL base for the applet.
	`archive="..."` Identifies the resources to be preloaded.
	`code="..."` The applet class file.
	`object="..."` The serialized applet file.
	`alt="..."` Displays text while loading.
	`name="..."` The name of the applet.
	`width="..."` The height of the displayed applet.
	`height="..."` The width of the displayed applet.

align="..." Deprecated. Controls alignment (left, center, right, justify).

hspace="..." The horizontal space separating the image from other content.

vspace="..." The vertical space separating the image from other content.

Empty   No.

Notes   Transitional DTD. Applet is deprecated in favor of the <object> element.

<img />

Usage   Includes an image in the document.

Start/End Tag   Required/Illegal.

Attributes   core, i18n, events.

src="..." The URL of the image.

alt="..." Alternative text to display.

align="..." Deprecated. Controls alignment (left, center, right, justify).

height="..." The height of the image.

width="..." The width of the image.

border="..." Border width.

hspace="..." The horizontal space separating the image from other content.

vspace="..." The vertical space separating the image from other content.

usemap="..." The URL to a client-side imagemap.

ismap="ismap"   Identifies a server-side imagemap.

Empty	Yes.
Notes	Strict DTD.

`<map>...</map>`

Usage	When used with the `<area>` element, creates a client-side imagemap.
Start/End Tag	Required/Required.
Attributes	core.
	name="..." The name of the imagemap to be created.
Empty	No.
Notes	Strict DTD.

`<object>...</object>`

Usage	Includes an object.
Start/End Tag	Required/Required.
Attributes	core, i18n, events.
	declare="declare" A flag that declares but doesn't create an object.
	classid="..." The URL of the object's location.
	codebase="..." The URL for resolving URLs specified by other attributes.
	data="..." The URL to the object's data.

`type="..."`   The Internet content type for data.

`codetype="..."`   The Internet content type for the code.

`standby="..."`   Show message while loading.

`align="..."`   Deprecated. Controls alignment (`left`, `center`, `right`, `justify`).

`height="..."`   The height of the object.

`width="..."`   The width of the object.

`border="..."`   Displays the border around an object.

`hspace="..."`   The space between the sides of the object and other page content.

`vspace="..."`   The space between the top and bottom of the object and other page content.

`usemap="..."`   The URL to an imagemap.

`shapes=`   Enables you to define areas to search for hyperlinks if the object is an image.

`name="..."`   The URL to submit as part of a form.

`tabindex="..."`   Sets the tabbing order between elements with a defined `tabindex`.

Empty	No.
Notes	Strict DTD. This element is new to HTML 4.

Style

Style sheets (both inline and external) are incorporated into an HTML document through the use of the <style> element.

<style>...</style>

Usage	Creates an internal style sheet.
Start/End Tag	Required/Required.
Attributes	i18n.
	type="..." The Internet content type.
	media="..." Defines the destination medium (screen, print, projection, braille, speech, all).
	title="..." The title of the style.
Empty	No.
Notes	Strict DTD. Located in the <head> element.

Forms

> forms   *Forms* create an interface for the user to select options and return data to the Web server.

<button>...</button>

Usage	Creates a button.
Start/End Tag	Required/Required.
Attributes	core, i18n, events.

`name="..."` The button name.

`value="..."` The value of the button.

`type="..."` The button type (`button`, `sub-mit`, `reset`).

`disabled="..."` Sets the button state to disabled.

`tabindex="..."` Sets the tabbing order between elements with a defined `tabindex`.

`onfocus="..."` The event that occurs when the element receives focus.

`onblur="..."` The event that occurs when the element loses focus.

Empty	No.
Notes	Strict DTD. This element is new to HTML 4.

`<form>...</form>`

Usage	Creates a form that holds controls for user input.
Start/End Tag	Required/Required.
Attributes	`core`, `i18n`, `events`.

`action="..."` The URL for the server action.

`method="..."` The HTTP method (`get`, `post`). `get` is deprecated.

`enctype="..."` Specifies the MIME (Internet media type).

`onsubmit="..."` The intrinsic event that occurs when the form is submitted.

`onreset="..."`   The intrinsic event that occurs when the form is reset.

`target="..."`   Determines where the resource will be displayed (user-defined name, `_blank`, `_parent`, `_self`, `_top`).

`accept-charset="..."`   The list of character encodings.

Empty	No.
Notes	Strict DTD.

`<input />`

Usage	Defines controls used in forms.
Start/End Tag	Required/Illegal.
Attributes	`core, i18n, events.`

`type="..."`   The type of input control (`text`, `password`, `checkbox`, `radio`, `submit`, `reset`, `file`, `hidden`, `image`, `button`).

`name="..."`   The name of the control (required except for `submit` and `reset`).

`value="..."`   The initial value of the control (required for radio and checkboxes).

`checked="checked"`   Sets the radio buttons to a checked state.

`disabled="..."`   Disables the control.

`readonly="..."`   For text password types.

`size="..."`   The width of the control in pixels except for text and password controls, which are specified in number of characters.

`maxlength="..."` The maximum number of characters that can be entered.

`src="..."` The URL to an image control type.

`alt="..."` An alternative text description.

`usemap="..."` The URL to a client-side imagemap.

`align="..."` Deprecated. Controls alignment (`left`, `center`, `right`, `justify`).

`tabindex="..."` Sets the tabbing order between elements with a defined `tabindex`.

`onfocus="..."` The event that occurs when the element receives focus.

`onblur="..."` The event that occurs when the element loses focus.

`onselect="..."` Intrinsic event that occurs when the control is selected.

`onchange="..."` Intrinsic event that occurs when the control is changed.

`accept="..."` File types allowed for upload.

Empty	Yes.
Notes	Strict DTD.

`<isindex />`

Usage	Prompts the user for input.
Start/End Tag	Required/Illegal.
Attributes	`core`, `i18n`.

prompt="..."   Provides a prompt string for
the input field.

Empty	Yes.
Notes	Transitional DTD. Deprecated.

`<label>...</label>`

Usage	Labels a control.
Start/End Tag	Required/Required.
Attributes	core, i18n, events.

for="..."   Associates a label with an identified control.

disabled="..."   Disables a control.

accesskey="..."   Assigns a hotkey to this
element.

onfocus="..."   The event that occurs when
the element receives focus.

onblur="..."   The event that occurs when
the element loses focus.

Empty	No.
Notes	Strict DTD. This element is new to HTML 4.

`<legend>...</legend>`

Usage	Assigns a caption to a FIELDSET.
Start/End Tag	Required/Required.
Attributes	core, i18n, events.

`align="..."`   Deprecated. Controls alignment (left, center, right, justify).

`accesskey="..."`   Assigns a hotkey to this
element.

Empty   No.

Notes   Strict DTD. This element is new to HTML 4.

`<option>...</option>`

Usage   Specifies choices in a `<select>` element.

Start/End Tag   Required/Optional.

Attributes   core, i18n, events.

`selected="selected"`   Specifies whether the
option is selected.

`disabled="disabled"`   Disables control.

`value="..."`   The value submitted if a control is submitted.

Empty   No.

Notes   Strict DTD.

`<select>...</select>`

Usage   Creates choices for the user to select.

Start/End Tag   Required/Required.

Attributes   core, i18n, events.

`name="..."`   The name of the element.

`size="..."`   The width in number of rows.

`multiple="multiple"`   Allows multiple
selections.

disabled="disabled" Disables the control.

tabindex="..." Sets the tabbing order between elements with a defined tabindex.

onfocus="..." The event that occurs when the element receives focus.

onblur="..." The event that occurs when the element loses focus.

onselect="..." Intrinsic event that occurs when the control is selected.

onchange="..." Intrinsic event that occurs when the control is changed.

Empty	No.
Notes	Strict DTD.

`<textarea>...</textarea>`

Usage	Creates an area for user input with multiple lines.
Start/End Tag	Required/Required.
Attributes	core, i18n, events.

name="..." The name of the control.

rows="..." The width in number of rows.

cols="..." The height in number of columns.

disabled="disabled" Disables the control.

readonly="readonly" Sets the displayed text to read-only status.

tabindex="..." Sets the tabbing order between elements with a defined tabindex.

`onfocus="..."`   The event that occurs when the element receives focus.

`onblur="..."`   The event that occurs when the element loses focus.

`onselect="..."`   Intrinsic event that occurs when the control is selected.

`onchange="..."`   Intrinsic event that occurs when the control is changed.

Empty	No.
Notes	Strict DTD. Text to be displayed is placed within the start and end tags.

Scripts

Scripting language is made available to process data and perform other dynamic events through the `<script>` element.

`<script>...</script>`

Usage	The `<script>` element contains client-side scripts that are executed by the browser.
Start/End Tag	Required/Required.
Attributes	`type="..."` Script language Internet content type.
	`language="..."` Deprecated. The scripting language, deprecated in favor of the `type` attribute.
	`src="..."` The URL for the external script.
Empty	No.
Notes	Strict DTD. You can set the default scripting language in the `<meta />` element.

`<noscript>...</noscript>`

Usage	Provides alternative content for browsers unable to execute a script.
Start/End Tag	Required/Required.
Attributes	None.
Empty	No.
Notes	Strict DTD. This element is new to HTML 4.

Common Attributes and Events

Four attributes are abbreviated as core in the preceding sections. They are:

- `id="..."` A global identifier.

- `class="..."` A list of classes separated by spaces.

- `style="..."` Style information.

- `title="..."` Provides more information for a specific element, as opposed to the `<title>` element, which entitles the entire Web page.

Two attributes for internationalization (i18n) are abbreviated as i18n:

- `lang="..."` The language identifier.

- `dir="..."` The text direction (`ltr`, `rtl`).

The following intrinsic events are abbreviated events:

- `OnClick="..."` A pointing device (such as a mouse) was single-clicked.

- `OnDblClick="..."` A pointing device (such as a mouse) was double-clicked.

- `OnMouseDown="..."` A mouse button was clicked and held down.

- `OnMouseUp="..."` A mouse button that was clicked and held down was released.

- `OnMouseOver="..."` A mouse moved the cursor over an object.

- `OnMouseMove="..."` The mouse was moved.

- `OnMouseOut="..."` A mouse moved the cursor off an object.

- `OnKeyPress="..."` A key was pressed and released.

- `OnKeyDown="..."` A key was pressed and held down.

- `OnKeyUp="..."` A key that was pressed has been released.

INDEX

U

mcp.com

The Authoritative Encyclopedia of Computing

Resource Centers
Books & Software
Personal Bookshelf
WWW Yellow Pages
Online Learning
Special Offers
Site Search
Industry News

▶ *Choose the online ebooks that you can view from your personal workspace on our site.*

About MCP   Site Map   Product Support

Turn to the *Authoritative* Encyclopedia of Computing

You'll find over 150 full text books online, hundreds of shareware/freeware applications, online computing classes and 10 computing resource centers full of expert advice from the editors and publishers of:

- Adobe Press
- BradyGAMES
- Cisco Press
- Hayden Books
- Lycos Press
- New Riders

- Que
- Que Education & Training
- Sams Publishing
- Waite Group Press
- Ziff-Davis Press

mcp.com
The Authoritative Encyclopedia of Computing

When you're looking for computing information, consult the authority. The Authoritative Encyclopedia of Computing at mcp.com.

Get the best information and learn about latest developments in:

■ Design

■ Graphics and Multimedia

■ Enterprise Computing and DBMS

■ General Internet Information

■ Operating Systems

■ Networking and Hardware

■ PC and Video Gaming

■ Productivity Applications

■ Programming

■ Web Programming and Administration

■ Web Publishing

SAMS Teach Yourself in 10 Minutes

Quick steps for fast results™

Sams Teach Yourself in 10 Minutes *gets you the results you want—fast! Work through the 10-minute lessons and learn everything you need to know quickly and easily. It's the handiest resource for the information you're looking for.*

Sams Teach Yourself Microsoft FrontPage 2000 in 10 Minutes

Galen A. Grimes
ISBN: 0-672-31498-3
$12.99 US/$19.95 CAN

Other Sams Teach Yourself in 10 Minutes Titles

Microsoft Publisher 2000
Joseph W. Habraken
ISBN: 0-672-31569-6
$12.99 US/$19.95 CAN

Microsoft Outlook 2000
Joseph W. Habraken
ISBN: 0-672-31450-9
$12.99 US/$19.95 CAN

Microsoft Internet Explorer 5
Jill T. Freeze
ISBN: 0-672-31646-3
$12.99 US/$19.95 CAN

Microsoft Office 2000
Laura Acklen
ISBN: 0-672-31431-2
$12.99 US/$19.95 CAN

Microsoft Word 2000
Peter G. Aitken
ISBN: 0-672-31441-x
$12.99 US/$19.95 CAN

Microsoft Excel 2000
Jennifer Fulton
ISBN: 0-672-31457-6
$12.99 US/$19.95 CAN

All prices are subject to change.

SAMS

www.samspublishing.com